Praise for *Growing Influence*

"This is not your typical leadership book. *Growing Influence* delivers fresh, insightful principles in a way that prompts deep introspection and inspires action. Prepare to grow alongside the characters."

—**Abbey Louie,** founder, Élan Consulting Group

"This book captures the heart of leadership. Ron and Stacy provide a clear road map to lead and grow your influence from a place of integrity and authenticity. Women and men will both benefit from the authors' experience and guidance."

—**Amanda Visosky,** program director and leadership coach,
Idaho Women in Leadership

"*Growing Influence* is an excellent read for those who feel stuck at any stage or level of their career. Approachable and insightful, this business fable provides both spiritual nourishment for the corporate soul as well as practical strategies for how to take back control over your career and parlay that into a purpose you are enthused about. It's an especially good read for rising stars who have hit barriers created by the 20th century fixed mindsets purported by those who still use a 'management' style approach to leading people. *Growing Influence* is clearly ushering in the next generation of truly accountable and empowered self-leadership."

—**Emily Soccorsy,** cofounder, Root + River

"*Growing Influence* weaves an accessible story using allegory and addresses timely issues about character and intergenerational communication. Using story and connection, this book tells the tale of empathy and mentorship and reminds us that sometimes we find the greatest gifts for our work in the most unexpected places."

—**Courtney Feider,** behavioral strategist and executive coach

"*Growing Influence* uses the #metoo theme to teach all of us how to have a more positive influence and greater success in our careers, marriages, and families. Whether you are a CEO or just starting down the leadership path, *Growing Influence* provides practical principles that can transform leaders, their teams, and the companies they work for. The book provides a tutorial for success through positive influence if you work hard, have talent, and are committed—whether you are female or male, young or old, or any ethnicity."

—**Rick Stott,** CEO, Superior Farms

GROWING INFLUENCE

A STORY OF HOW TO LEAD WITH
CHARACTER, EXPERTISE, AND IMPACT

———

RON PRICE AND STACY ENNIS

GREENLEAF
BOOK GROUP PRESS

Published by Greenleaf Book Group Press
Austin, Texas
www.gbgpress.com

Distributed by Greenleaf Book Group

For ordering information or special discounts for bulk purchases, please contact Greenleaf Book Group at PO Box 91869, Austin, TX 78709, 512.891.6100.

Design and composition by Greenleaf Book Group and Kim Lance
Cover design by Greenleaf Book Group and Kim Lance
Cover image: ©Thinkstock / iStock Collection / vwPix

Publisher's Cataloging-in-Publication data is available.

Print ISBN: 978-1-62634-557-7

eBook ISBN: 978-1-62634-558-4

Part of the Tree Neutral® program, which offsets the number of trees consumed in the production and printing of this book by taking proactive steps, such as planting trees in direct proportion to the number of trees used: www.treeneutral.com

Printed in the United States of America on acid-free paper

19 20 21 22 23 24   11 10 9 8 7 6 5 4 3 2

First Edition

To the women and men who care enough
about becoming great leaders that they will
conquer every obstacle along the way.

Contents

1   The Encounter   1

2   You Have Influence   9

3   Where Should I Focus?   31

4   For Now, Ignore Position   51

5   Character First   65

6   Who I Want to Become   89

7   Next, Become an Expert   101

8   Let's Talk about Structural Leadership   113

9   What Great Leaders Do   145

10   It's Time   157

Acknowledgments   *169*

Resources   *171*

Reader's Guide   *173*

Q&A with the Authors   *175*

About the Authors   *183*

1

The Encounter

mily watched the barista with growing urgency as he steamed the water and then walked over to a set of three empty glass coffee funnels and decanters. He placed a filter over the middle funnel, tipped the water over the filter, and looked at Emily, pushing his square glasses up.

"We do this to clean the filter," he said. "Makes better coffee."

She offered a half-smile and checked her watch, which was buzzing from the emails already coming in. Shifting her weight—her laptop bag felt especially heavy that morning—she ran a hand through her dark brown hair, twisting it briefly before letting it fall, a nervous habit she'd picked up in adulthood. She looked out the window. When she glanced back in the direction of the barista, he was steaming more water. With a grimace, she looked at her watch again as he scooped coffee grounds into the filter.

Scoop, dump, scoop, dump, scoop, dump. Sigh.

He walked to the back counter to retrieve the steaming water and poured it over the grounds with an impressive slowness. The coffee drip-drip-dripped into the waiting glass container. Emily let out a subtle but exasperated breath.

"I can bring this to your table," the barista said. "That's what we normally do."

Now you tell me, she thought, as she said aloud, "Great."

Emily rushed up the stairs and unloaded the contents of her work bag onto the long oak table. She opened her laptop, set out her notes, and pulled up her presentation file before checking her watch again.

Scrolling through the slides, she felt confident. She told herself it was going to go perfectly—she was prepared, well rested, and had even gotten a workout in that morning, not to mention the bike ride to the coffee shop. Now, she just needed to do final preparations. But as Emily scrolled to the fourteenth slide, she paused, panicked. The slide was blank. Where was the text she'd put in the night before?

Hastily, she continued scrolling. Slides fifteen, sixteen, seventeen—they were all blank.

With growing panic, she began looking through her handwritten notes. She would have to recreate the presentation. But first, she closed her eyes and took a deep breath, then another.

"Here you go."

Emily jumped at the voice behind her. She laughed nervously. "Smells delicious. Thanks."

The barista set the coffee on the table to her right as Emily began remaking the presentation she was set to give in an hour and forty minutes. Those slides had taken her nearly three hours to create the first time; hopefully she'd be able to whip them together before the meeting. So much for the additional prep she'd planned to do that morning.

Emily reached for the coffee, her eyes still on her screen. A second later, hot liquid was all over the table. She scooped up her laptop and notes just in time.

"Dang it, dang it, dang it." After relocating her items to the other end of the table, she turned around to search for napkins, nearly colliding with someone. She jumped back as a man extended a stack of napkins.

"Looking for these?" he said.

"Oh, yeah. Thanks." She paused momentarily before smiling and taking the stack from him. The man went to grab more napkins and then walked over to help mop up the mess.

"Here, I'll take the wet towels," he offered, gathering up the dripping paper.

"Thank you."

As Emily finished drying the table, all she could think about was her presentation. She set to work getting her area reorganized.

The man returned from throwing away the second set of wet towels. "All dry?"

Emily looked up from her work space and surveyed the man in front of her. He had neatly styled white hair and wore a button-up shirt, tailored jeans, and brown leather dress shoes. His eyes wrinkled into a genuine smile just as Emily realized how odd it must seem that she was standing there staring at him. She smiled back.

"Yes, thanks so much."

He nodded and reached out his hand. "I'm David."

"David. I'm Emily." She shook his hand. "Thanks, again."

"Of course." He looked toward her ordered workstation. "May I ask what you're working on?"

"I have a big presentation in"—she checked her watch and lifted her eyebrows in surprise—"an hour and a half. If you'll excuse me, I need to get back to work."

"Of course." David made his way back to his table, which was directly across from hers. He picked up his tablet, returning to the news article he'd been reading.

Over the next hour, Emily focused intently on her computer screen, her hands moving furiously. With five minutes to spare, she saved the file three times just to be sure. Finally, she gathered her items, placed them in her bag, and rushed out the door without looking back. She didn't realize David was watching her the whole time.

—

"Good job today," Mitchell said. The conference room had cleared out, and Emily was gathering her presentation materials. She still felt the familiar rush of an excellent presentation—her mind sharp, body energized, breathing a bit shallower than normal. She smiled at Mitchell.

"Do you think they're on board with how artificial intelligence can transform our business?"

"It's hard to say. They've been doing things the same way for years."

"True."

The room grew quiet. Mitchell lingered as Emily cleaned up.

"You know, I've been wanting to know—" Emily said.

"There's something I'd like to—" Mitchell began.

"You first," Emily said.

"Well, we both know you were up for a promotion."

"Right." Emily sensed what was coming next. Discussions never start that way when you've gotten the job. "I'm excited to be considered."

"You've been wowing everyone on this Asia project, myself included, with your hard work. Honestly, you're one of the best I've seen."

"Well, thank you. This past month has been a good challenge."

"And you've tackled the challenge head-on"—he paused, looking at the table before raising his eyes to meet hers—"but I don't think you're quite ready for the next step."

"What?" She startled herself with this response. Get it together, she thought.

"We've given the promotion to Stan."

Stan? Stan, the same guy she'd started her trainee program with—the one who'd just received terrible ratings in his latest customer response survey and showed up late to meetings? Seriously?

"I see. Thanks for letting me know. So if I can ask, what am I missing?"

Mitchell stretched his mouth into an attempted smile. "It'll be your time soon. I meant what I said. You're doing great."

"I appreciate that."

"OK, then." Mitchell knocked lightly on the desk twice. "See you at 2 p.m. for our team meeting."

"See you."

Emily hung back in the conference room. She sat at the head of the table, her elbows on the surface, hands together in a fist and forehead resting on her hands. Then she leaned back and stared at the ceiling.

This was the third promotion she'd been passed over for. She thought about the people who'd received promotions over the past two years: James, Kyle, Stan. She had gone through the same manager trainee program with them—they'd all been hired at the same time, started on the same day, and were deploying different parts of the same product. What gives?

Over the past month, she'd been watching the company's monthly metrics. Her team had far surpassed Stan's in customer acquisition, retention, and satisfaction. They launched updates faster with fewer bugs, while Stan's team had been slowing down with launches and reporting more issues with their code. Her direct reports consistently praised her leadership, and while she liked Stan, she'd heard the rumblings of dissent within his team. It had been a similar story with James and Kyle. And yet they had gotten promotions and she hadn't.

The last time this had happened, a good friend had suggested it might be because she's a woman. Emily had rejected the idea at the time, but now she wasn't so sure. She wanted to believe her confidence and intelligence outweighed centuries of bias, but she also didn't want to be naïve. It seemed there were too many signs to ignore.

She'd worked for nearly a decade at this company, and now she felt stagnant. After missing the last promotion, she'd even gone to the lengths of conducting her own version of a 360 review, in which she solicited anonymous feedback from nearly a dozen people on her team and in her network. A few comments had stung—two people said she was too direct and unemotional, one said she had trouble fully delegating projects—but otherwise they were overwhelmingly positive. She couldn't identify anything serious enough to be holding her back from getting promoted, and she'd been actively working to improve on issues called out during the review. One of the other managers had even made a comment about how well she'd delegated on a recent project, which had given her confidence that she was improving.

Emily shifted her attention to the ten executive chairs askew in the room. She sighed, then stood and walked to each chair, pushing them in. Three dirty coffee cups were on the table, and she gathered them one at a time. Someone had spilled a dime-sized coffee puddle, and as she retrieved a napkin from the beverage station at the back of the room, she stopped.

She stood there, three coffee cups in one hand and a napkin in the other. It had been ten years since she'd been the new manager trainee, and yet here she was, cleaning up after her colleagues and bosses like their mom. She did enough of that at home with her own child.

Emily walked around the table and set each coffee cup back where it had been, then made her way over to the beverage station and returned the napkin.

"I have begun my own quiet war," she whispered, reciting a section from her favorite book, *The House on Mango Street*. "Simple. Sure. I am the one who leaves the table like a man, without putting back the chair or picking up the plate."

She looked at the spilled coffee on the table with defiance, slung her bag over her shoulder, and walked out of the room.

2

You Have Influence

Emily stood outside the renovated brick building, the aroma of gourmet coffee tempting her into Slow by Slow. She'd been craving their pour-over coffee since she'd had her first cup the week before—before she gave the presentation of her life, before she was passed over for a promotion she knew she deserved. Emily's shoulders tightened as she remembered the conversation in the conference room. Why hadn't she simply asked Mitchell why he'd given the promotion to Stan? Why hadn't she advocated for herself?

Within minutes, Emily had ordered her coffee and was making her way upstairs to a table. It was busy this morning—not exactly the tranquil work space she had hoped for—but she had come prepared. She dug into her bag and pulled out two earplugs, accessories she never left home without. After the plugs were situated in her ears, she took a breath, relaxed her shoulders, and opened up the file she'd be delivering to her team that afternoon. When her coffee arrived, she smiled her thanks and carefully moved the mug into her line of sight, just out of the laptop spill zone.

Half an hour rushed by. Emily's watch buzzed, reminding her of a meeting in an hour. There was still plenty of time before she needed to leave, and she was almost done with her work. Ten minutes later, she was finished, with time to spare. Or maybe, she thought as she stifled a yawn, time for a refill.

Emily stood and made her way to the lower level of the shop to get a refill, another yawn edging its way toward her lips. Her son had woken up screaming the night before—he'd heard a "bump, bump, bump," he'd told her, whimpering between tears, his chest heaving—and it had taken thirty minutes to get him calmed and to sleep, then another forty-five to fall asleep herself. When her alarm went off at 5:30, it had been just short of painful. OK, it had been painful.

"Want a refill?" the barista asked. Emily couldn't help but admire the barista's cropped auburn hair and no-makeup look.

"Please. Just drip this time."

"Sure thing." The barista walked to the back counter and filled Emily's cup, then walked back to Emily and handed it over.

"Thanks."

The woman nodded. "Hey, you've been in before, right? You look familiar."

Emily laughed. "Once. I spilled coffee everywhere. I like to make an impression."

"Right! Well, be careful with this one." She grinned.

Drink in hand, Emily made her way back to her table. She stopped abruptly when a friendly pair of eyes met hers.

"Emily, right?" It was the man who'd helped her clean up the coffee mess the week before. It took her a moment to respond as she considered the strange coincidence of running into him right after talking about the coffee fiasco. But, she reminded herself, she didn't believe in coincidences.

"Good memory," Emily replied. "Dan, right?"

"Close. David," he said. He stood, walking over to her with an outstretched hand. Emily was surprised to realize he was much taller than her—well over six feet to her five feet five inches.

"David," she said, grasping his hand. "Nice to see you. Do you come here often?"

"Every day. Well, every morning. Shortly after I retired, my wife told me she needed me to get out of the house more, so I found somewhere to go on the weekdays." He gestured around the coffee house. "I love it here."

"It's growing on me."

"I'm surprised you came back after last time. You seemed—"

"—stressed? Overwhelmed? Frustrated?"

David laughed. "Well, yeah. Something like that."

"The coffee drew me back," Emily replied, a slight grin on her face.

He met her eyes, his expression softening. "If you don't mind me asking, is everything better now?"

Emily almost laughed out loud in surprise at his question. She surveyed him for a half second, her wide blue eyes taking in his hazel ones, unsure of how to respond. Finally, she waved her hand, brushing off his concern. "Oh, yeah. Yep. Everything's fine." She hardly knew this person and wasn't about to share her disappointing boardroom experience from the week before.

"Good. You seemed focused on something important."

"I was. But it's done now. On to the next. Isn't that how it always works in corporate America?"

"Oh, corporate. Yes, I'm familiar with that world." David's eyes grew unfocused, as though looking through Emily to another time. She almost asked about his background but held back her inquisitiveness.

"Well, tech corporate. I guess it's pretty close to the rest of the corporate world."

"I suppose you're right. Can I ask you another question?"

Emily hesitated, but curiosity won. "Sure."

"Are you happy where you're at? Do you feel like you're fulfilling what you're meant to in life?"

Emily looked at him in disbelief, startled at the bluntness of the question. There was a long silence as she decided how to answer. Who was this stranger, and where did he get off asking such personal questions?

Still, it was a question she knew she needed to answer, at least for herself. She felt a rush of frustration from the top of her head down the length of her spine—not because of the man in front of her, but from the last months, years even, at her company. Happy in life? Yes. Happy in work? No. Not even close.

She had been talking about the barely missed promotions to her husband and friends, but none of them had offered a helpful perspective. In fact, the conversations had felt circular. They had all commiserated with her, offering support but not much else. She needed to know what to *do*.

The weight of the stretching silence finally pulled Emily out of thought. She realized she was standing in the middle of a newly familiar coffee shop contemplating a personal question asked by a man she'd met briefly one time. He was watching her, waiting. Yes, this was an odd scenario, and yet something about the exchange felt comfortable.

"Well, I"—her watch buzzed, and Emily snapped out of almost sharing her private work challenges with a stranger—"I have to go. Nice seeing you again."

"You too, Emily."

She lingered for a moment, about to speak, but held back. Finally, she offered a polite smile and walked back to her table to gather her things. Out of the corner of her eye, she saw David make his way back to his own table, sit down, and pick up his tablet. As she placed each item in her bag, Emily realized how close she'd come to baring her soul. Unemotional Emily, as her close friends called her, didn't do things like that. The nickname wasn't fair, though. Emily felt things deeply; she just didn't show it very often or to people she didn't trust.

As she walked toward the stairs to exit the coffee shop, she turned to offer a tight wave.

"See you soon," David replied, waving.

"Yep. See you," Emily called back as she descended the steps.

That was strange, she thought. Very strange.

Her bicycle was parked outside the shop, and she unlocked the chain and put her helmet on. Despite the strangely personal question, she couldn't help feeling as though David was someone she should get to know. He was old enough to be her dad, and yet the way he talked to her didn't feel fatherly. Their short exchange had been like connecting with an old friend.

Emily rode the half-mile to work, locked up her bike, and looked up at the building she'd worked at for the past ten years. She took a breath and closed her eyes.

Today will be better, she thought. It has to be.

She opened her eyes, pushed aside her morning exchange at the coffee shop, and walked inside.

———

Precisely one week later, Emily found herself outside Slow by Slow. She hadn't planned to go there, and yet somehow her bicycle had pedaled its way to what was becoming her favorite coffee shop. She looked at the door, which was propped open to welcome the cool April morning air. He was inside—she just knew it. It seemed her bicycle knew it, too. She set about locking her frame to the bike stand and removing her helmet, getting ready to head inside.

Since her last discussion with David, she hadn't stopped thinking about his question: Do you feel like you're fulfilling what you're meant to in life? The answer, quite simply, was no. No, she wasn't fulfilling her purpose in life. She wasn't even fulfilling her purpose within the company. On top of that, she'd been working extra-long hours gearing up for a product launch, with little to show for her dedication. She missed her family, her friends, her cat. She was tired and not getting enough exercise, let alone the mental space she needed to function at her best. Last week alone, she put in eighty-two hours, and that wasn't including the time she spent catching up on email after arriving home at 9 p.m.

She'd gone through a loop of emotion: anger, frustration, dejection, begrudging acceptance, and back to anger. And it wasn't just the promotion—it was the work environment in general. Despite her talent and hard work, she felt powerless. And that powerlessness seemed to be shoved in her face every day, from little things like being forced to sit toward the back of the room during a meeting because the front chairs were all taken (by men), to her boss, Mitchell, pitching her idea to the executive team without giving her credit.

She wasn't an angry person, but she felt like one lately. She'd even snapped at little Henry last night during his now-regular night waking, an occurrence she suspected had something to do with the fact that she was gone so much. He just wanted to see his mama, she knew, and feel loved. And she couldn't even give him that.

To combat her emotional loop, Emily kept reminding herself that she needed to be grateful. With a secure job and great income, shouldn't she just put her head down and deal with it? Still, every thought of work was accompanied by a steady uneasiness in her gut.

"What are you doing?" A small voice snapped Emily out of her thoughtful daze. She looked down at a young girl, who was staring up at Emily in wonder. The girl's long, dark lashes contrasted with her golden blonde curls and light blue Superwoman shirt. The child stood, unblinking, looking at Emily in wonder. It was at that moment that Emily realized she had her helmet in one hand and was, once again, staring at the coffee shop door. She laughed.

"Thinking," Emily replied.

"About what?"

"Grace," the girl's mother said, "let her be."

"It's OK," Emily replied. "I was thinking about happiness." That was kind of true, she reasoned. Or at least it was a positive spin on the negative cycle of thoughts she couldn't seem to break.

The girl giggled and ran off, and the mom offered the sacred smile mothers offer each other in such moments. Emily smiled back.

Soon after, Emily had placed her order and walked up the stairs to find a table. She caught sight of David, who was sitting in the back corner reading his tablet, and walked over to him.

"Good morning, David," she said, sure to get his name right this time.

"Emily! Good to see you." He motioned to the chair across from him. "Want to join me?"

"Sure. Thanks," she replied, not quite sure what she was doing or why she was so drawn to talk to this gentleman. As she sat, the barista brought her coffee, and Emily gathered it between her hands, warming her palms after the chilly bike ride.

"Last time I saw you, we got cut off in our conversation," David said. "Mind if we resume it?"

He didn't waste time, Emily mused. "Yeah, sorry about that. I had to get to work. And to be honest, you caught me on an especially frustrating day."

"Why's that?"

"Well"—Emily hesitated, looking at her coffee and then back at David—"work has just been . . . frustrating."

"You said that already," David replied, his voice gentle. He set his tablet down and removed his glasses—trendy, square black frames Emily assumed were for reading.

"Right. It's hard to put into words."

"Well, how about we start with this: Where do you work?"

Finally, a question she could easily answer. "I work at Enertec. It's a sustainability tech company, and we're working on building software that runs renewable energy machines like wind turbines and smart watering systems for farmers. Have you heard of the Industrial Internet of Things?"

"I have. Can't say I understand it, though."

"Basically, we add computation and sensors to machines that are connected to the Internet so that we can gather and monitor data."

"Sounds pretty exciting."

"It is. I love what we're working on, but my boss . . . well, not so much."

"Oh?"

Emily thought of Mitchell. He wasn't so bad. She didn't feel angry at him, exactly, more at the system that had trained him.

"Last time I saw you, he'd just passed me up for a promotion." Emily hesitated before continuing, eyeing the man in front of her. He had a kind face—genuine, much like her husband, only with more years of wisdom. She decided to trust her instinct and share the real story, or at least the light version of it. "It just . . . it feels like I'm not being recognized for my hard work, diligence, how I work with my team. All of it."

David nodded his head in understanding. "I'm sorry. I've been there, both being passed over myself and as the boss doing the passing over. It's never easy."

"Definitely not easy."

"Mind if I offer some advice?"

What do I have to lose? she thought. Worst-case scenario, this conversation gets awkward, and I'll have to avoid this coffee shop so I won't run into him. Best-case scenario, he has good advice that can actually help.

"Sure," she replied.

David slid his empty coffee cup to the end of the table and rested his elbows on the oak surface, clasping his hands together. He sat up a bit straighter, and his gaze grew sharp. Emily couldn't help but picture him in an executive boardroom, addressing a group of twenty-five senior leaders about company strategy.

"What I'm hearing you say is that you don't feel noticed or influential in your company," he began. "And from my experience, people who feel that way are often frustrated, disillusioned, and at odds with their environment. The culture, leadership, or something else makes them feel like they can't be the best version of themselves."

Emily listened in a state of both awe and disbelief. It felt like he was detailing her very experience at Enertec. And yet, she wondered, could he really understand what it meant to be a woman in a male-dominated field, to be passed over for things due to biases outside her control? Almost as soon as those thoughts came, though, she pushed them away. She was determined to not let her dissatisfaction cloud their conversation.

David went on to explain that people who feel like they have influence at work feel affirmed and highly engaged. They go the second or third mile, and they just keep going, like an upward spiral of things getting better and better.

"You're using 'influence' differently than I've heard it before," Emily said. "I usually hear it in reference to celebrities or politicians. How would you define it?"

"There are a lot of definitions, but the one I like best is 'the capacity or power to have an effect on someone or something.'"[1]

---

1   "Influence." *New Oxford American Dictionary.*

"That's exactly what I want. To have an effect. To feel like I have some power at work."

"What if you could have influence in every situation? What if you always felt like you had influence at work?"

"Sounds nice, but unrealistic. There's no way that's going to happen in my current situation."

"Actually, there is a possibility to have influence, even at Enertec."

Emily raised her eyebrows. "How?"

"In order to share how, it's important to understand that there are three types of influence. Mind if I go through them?"

"Please." At this, Emily leaned forward.

David began with the first kind of influence, in which a person has 100 percent control over their situation. Nobody can block someone from having influence in this area, and yet if they fail to influence, there's nobody to blame but themselves.

"What's an example?" Emily asked.

"Well, do you think you can exercise 100 percent control over what time you get up in the morning?" David responded.

Emily laughed. "If Henry, my son, will let me sleep for once."

"Fair enough. I remember those years. But you still have control over whether you sleep in or wake up early, no matter how exhausted you are. Correct?" Emily nodded, and David went on. "In your work, where's the possibility that you could have 100 percent control?"

Emily was quiet. She thought for several seconds. "Honestly, I don't know. I get interrupted all the time, projects get changed—I feel like I'm at the mercy of upper management who has no idea what's going on with our team."

"What about discretionary time?" David said.

"Wouldn't that be nice."

"What if I told you that even as a CEO running a global company, I found four hours of discretionary time every morning?"

"Four hours?" Emily repeated. She stared in disbelief as she registered the fact that she was sitting with the former CEO of a global organization who had found four hours every single day for discretionary time. Clearly, this was someone to listen to.

"Yes, four hours. What if I could show you how to carve out time in your day, too?"

"I'd love that."

David explained that early in his career, he had a set of cassette tapes sitting on his shelf that he'd been meaning to listen to for months. Ironically, the set was about time management. One day, a friend told him she'd listened to the whole set and how great the information was—it had transformed her workday. That same evening, David had decided that no one was going to make time for him to listen to the tapes; he had to find the time himself. The next morning, he went into work an hour early and listened to a cassette tape, taking notes. Soon after, he came in two hours early, using some of the time for learning and some for strategy development and thinking. By the end of his career at the company, he was arriving at 6:00 a.m. every day, and he had discretionary time until 10:00 a.m. He'd even left many days at 4:00 p.m. to make it to his kids' sports games.

"For four hours every day, I could be focused and present," David said. "I advanced as a leader and gave more of myself to the company because I could think and plan more strategically."

"And how did your boss and team react?" Emily replied. "It sounds like you were technically putting in less 'on the clock' time, but you were working more hours."

"Well, sort of. I used some of that discretionary time for personal development, but I also spent hours on strategy development, writing, and other tasks related to my position that I needed to do uninterrupted. Once I was promoted to CEO, I technically only had to answer to the owners and board, but the perception of my team was even more important to me. It took a while, but soon they began to see the benefit of my focused time. I got more done, faster, and I was able to be fully present when I was in meetings because my mind wasn't on the six things I needed to finish by the end of the day."

"I never thought of it that way. But wow, four hours? I don't think I could do that."

"It doesn't have to be four hours. Do you think you could find fifteen minutes of discretionary time?"

"I'm pretty sure I can find thirty. I think I'll start going in half an hour early."

"That's great, but here's the key. You have to educate the people around you that it's your time. I had to teach my assistant and the rest of my team. They knew that short of a fire, they were not to disturb me. Trust me when I say that, pretty soon, people are going to realize you're coming in early. You've got to tell them you own that time and don't want to be interrupted. And that means you're also going to have to tell your boss."

Emily let out a breath. "OK. I can do that."

"That's the first type of influence: control. At least once a day, you can feel that you have influence."

"This is excellent. You said there were three, right?" She leaned further forward.

David chuckled. "You're right. The second kind of influence is collaboration. It's about figuring out a way to collaborate with others who want something you also want. Do you think there are people in your company who want something you want?"

Emily considered his question, then said with a smirk, "Well, we all want promotions."

David shook his head, smiling. "OK, let me rephrase the question. Is there something lacking in the organization that everyone could use more of?"

Emily's expression turned thoughtful. She recalled the last meeting with her colleagues, other managers who led teams like hers. Mitchell had spent the bulk of the meeting picking apart the negative feedback from a recent customer satisfaction survey, and everyone had left dejected and frustrated. "You know, one thing that's lacking is encouragement. It's like everyone gets criticized when something goes wrong and we just take it for granted when something goes right. We don't celebrate successes. And I can think of a few people who would also like to see more positivity and encouragement."

"And how could you do that?"

"I mean, short of becoming the company cheerleader, I honestly don't know."

David tilted his head to the side and back slightly, as if challenging her statement. "No ideas?"

Emily was surprised at how quickly he'd dropped the I-just-met-you politeness. He was kind but frank, and the exchange felt comfortable and unforced.

"Influence through collaboration," she began, thinking aloud. "I know several people who would like to see more encouragement at work. Maybe we could meet together and come up with ideas on how we could spread an attitude of celebration in our organization."

"That's a great place to start," David said. "I like to call those efforts at collaboration a 'virtuous conspiracy.'"

"I love that," Emily said, grabbing her phone, opening up her notes app, and typing in *virtuous conspiracy*. She looked back up at David, her eyes bright. "I could see organizing a monthly lunch where we celebrate people who've done great work—we could surprise the people being honored. And it doesn't have to be limited to my team. I'd love to spread this celebratory spirit throughout the company."

"Great plan. Will you let me know how it goes?"

"You bet."

"Can't wait," David said, retrieving his coffee cup from the edge of the table. "Excuse me. I'm going to grab a refill. Would you like anything?" Emily shook her head no.

As David walked across the room and down the stairs, she checked her watch, realizing she needed to be at work in half an hour. Just then, something blue caught her eye—a debit card lying next to David's tablet. Emily tilted her head to read the name on the card: David Ford. Emily sat back up quickly, chiding herself for snooping, and then forgave herself. After all, if she was going to spend the morning with him, shouldn't she know his last name? She heard David chatting with the barista. It was several minutes before he made his way back to the table.

He'd hardly sat down when Emily resumed the discussion. "You said there was a third?"

"Ah, yes," David said, taking a drink of his fresh coffee. "Unfortunately, the third area is where you're going to feel the least amount of influence. We've covered the areas of control and collaboration, and now we're going to talk about the area of concern."

"Concern?" Emily's eyebrows drew sharply inward as she considered the word. "As in, this is a concerning area of influence?"

David laughed. "No, but I like your version. The area of concern is when you're worried about something going on in the company, or even outside of it, but you don't see how you can influence it. You might be able to influence it later, but today it's invisible to you how you might have influence."

"Hmm. What are some examples?"

"Is there something you're spending energy on—something you think about a lot that preoccupies or distracts you but you can't see a way to influence it right now?"

Their table was silent as Emily thought, but the coffee shop around them buzzed with energy and conversation. What was stealing her attention at work? What distracted or preoccupied her mental energy?

"One thing comes to mind," she finally said. "There are discussions that we might be acquired by another company, and that could ruin all my plans. We'll have a whole new set of leaders who don't know me. And from looking at their past acquisitions, there's a chance I might even end up without a job. It's just"—Emily looked at the ceiling and inhaled, exhaling as she looked back at David—"I'm worried. I don't know for sure if we'll be acquired because it's only rumors at this point, but I'm stressed about it."

"That's a great example of an area of concern. Any other examples?"

Emily thought for a moment. "Nothing I can think of."

"How do you feel about politics in America these days?"

"Don't get me started," Emily replied. "It's just falling apart. What kind of country—"

"Concern, Emily," David interrupted. Emily was surprised but intrigued. "That's another good example of an area of concern where your influence, if there is any at all, is invisible. It's not something you feel you can grab ahold of."

"So how is it an area of influence?"

"Well, you'll gain influence over time. At least with things that you have a connection to, like your company and the acquisition."

"How?"

"There's not a straightforward strategy, but I do know that which-ever of these areas of influence you focus on is going to grow—usu-ally at the expense of the others. You could think of each area like a circle: control, collaboration, and concern." David drew imaginary circles on the table with his right index finger as he spoke. "When one circle grows, another shrinks. With people I know who've really worked on building their circle of control, there's a proportionate shrinkage of their circle of concern. They haven't actually attacked the circle of concern; it's just that it's not stealing their power any-more. When you focus on control, especially when it comes to time, you also have more space to think of ideas for the area of collabora-tive influence. And interestingly, as control and collaboration grow, you might also discover influence in the area of concern that wasn't visible before."

Emily sat quietly, processing what David said. Instead of circles, she pictured three connected balloons; to grow one balloon, she'd have to take air from another. So, as control and collaboration grew, concern would get smaller. If discretionary time and creating a virtuous conspiracy were her focus, she'd have little time to fret over the acquisition.

"I think I see what you mean. When I focus on an area of control, like time, I have space to think more, to be more strategic and thoughtful. I can think creatively around how I can influence through collaboration and execute my part of the collaboration. And by giving my time and energy to control and collaboration, I stop worrying about the things I can't control, the area of concern."

"You've got it," David said. "And once you build influence in the other areas, you may also find that you do actually have some influence over the acquisition. The reality is you'll never get rid of the area of concern, but it becomes smaller because you're able to find opportunities to move those things you're concerned about into the area of collaboration or control."

"Interesting. I need to think on that a bit. Where did you learn all this, by the way?"

"You know, I first read about it in Stephen Covey's *The 7 Habits of Highly Effective People*. It's the first habit, which he calls 'Be Proactive,' and it's all about owning your future. He talks about the circle of influence and circle of concern. During my decades in leadership, I began to notice more nuance to influence, so I built on his idea with three areas of influence: control, collaboration, and concern. By the way, that'd be a great book for you to read."

Emily was already noting the title in her phone. "I will."

David broke his boardroom posture and eased back into his chair. "But look, these are just ideas. They worked for me and some of my friends, but I don't know if they'll work for you."

"I'll try anything," Emily said. "Control, collaboration, concern. Coming in thirty minutes early and starting a virtuous conspiracy around celebration."

"That has a nice ring to it," David said, his eyes wrinkling into a smile.

"Sure does," Emily agreed. "Well, I have to go. Work calls. I'll see you soon?"

"I'll be here."

Emily stood, placed her bag on her shoulder, and started to walk away. Then, she turned and walked back to the table. "Hey, thanks," she said. "You barely know me, and yet you gave me your whole morning."

"I'm retired, remember? I still have another three hours of my morning." He smiled. "But you're welcome."

———

Later that evening, after her son was in bed and her husband had gone into the garage to work on his bicycle, Emily settled into the living room couch with a glass of wine and her computer. Her cat walked over to the couch, leapt onto the cushions, and cozied up to Emily's right thigh.

She pulled up Google and typed in "David Ford Boise CEO." When nearly nine million results came up, she knew it was going to take a while to find information about him. She tried a combination of different phrases that she recalled from their conversation. Nothing. With a glance at the clock on her computer, she decided to give it ten more minutes and then call it a night.

Finally, Emily came across an article that read, "David Ford, CEO, Runs His Global Manufacturing Company with Pride and Perseverance." The piece included photos of a much younger David. She glanced at the date at the top of the article. It was written fourteen years ago.

In one photo, he stood overlooking his manufacturing plant from a second-story interior platform. He was serious and focused, his forearms resting on a railing that ran the length of the second floor. In another photo, he was mid-speech on stage in a packed meeting room of hundreds, the backs of their heads to the camera, David's right arm lifted into the air as though he were making a critical point. She scrolled down and saw another image of him at a wide mahogany desk, pen in hand as he signed a document. Two men stood at either side of him, staring at the paper he was signing. And finally, she saw a close-up image of him looking at the camera, a close-lipped smile on his face.

Emily was captivated as she read the article. It detailed his leadership and legacy at the company, complete with quotes from employees and people in the community. At one point, it read, he led over 5,000 employees in sixteen countries. He was portrayed as nearly heroic. Emily almost laughed at some of the writing, which was so over-the-top she couldn't help but wonder if his biggest fan had written the article. "When David walks into a room, voices hush, hearts still, and ears awaken," it read.

As Emily finished the article, she tried to stitch together coffee shop David with CEO David. She could see it—the sharp gaze, the years of knowledge he'd shared that morning—and yet, the two Davids seemed disconnected. In many ways, David could be any unassuming older gentleman at a coffee shop. She'd likely never have known of his success if she hadn't spilled her coffee that day.

Still, the article was comforting, because it validated what she'd felt in their first conversation: wisdom in his words and presence that made her want to get to know him more. Coming from the world of manufacturing, though, she wondered how much they could really have in common. His was a world of men doing men's work, a patriarchy she fought a quiet battle against every day in the tech world. There he was, in the article and photos, presiding over men. She couldn't find a single woman in any of the pictures. She wondered if he could fully understand what women deal with in the workplace.

Emily closed her laptop and sat in the stillness for several moments, lost in thought. A creaking sound brought her back as the door to the garage opened, and her husband walked through the kitchen and into the living room, where Emily sat.

"You OK?" Jason said. "Still thinking about the promotion?"

"You know what? No. For the first time in a while, no."

"I'm glad. Better day today?"

"In some ways. You know that guy I had coffee with this morning? The one I told you about earlier?"

"David, right?"

She nodded, then patted her computer. "I just read an interesting article about him. It was a profile about his role as CEO at a company based here in Boise."

"Really? Will you send it to me?"

"Of course." Emily yawned, set her laptop on the cushion, and stretched her arms, reaching past the back of the couch. Her cat lifted its head, looked at her with squinty eyes, and lay back down. When Emily stood to walk into the kitchen, it jumped off and ran across the room to find another place to sleep.

Before Emily could make it to the kitchen, Jason walked over and wrapped her in a hug. She held him for a moment before letting go. "Thanks for being here for me."

He kissed her forehead. "It's getting late."

She yawned. "Let's hope Henry lets us sleep for once."

"Unlikely."

"I know." The two made their way upstairs, walking quietly past Henry's room. Emily looked at the door, willing her boy to sleep all night but secretly looking forward to snuggling with him if he woke up. Minutes later, eyes wide open as she lay awake in the dark, she shook her head, marveling at the contradictions of motherhood and career.

Soon, with the comforter hugged close to her chin, she fell asleep.

3

Where Should I Focus?

mily set her bag down in her office and checked her watch. Eight o'clock. She typically arrived by eight thirty every day, and this was her first morning of discretionary time.

She pulled a journal and book out of her bag and set them on the desk. Then, she walked over to her office window, drew the blinds, and returned to her seat. This morning, she would spend fifteen minutes journaling and fifteen minutes reading. She'd purchased a new journal and *The 7 Habits of Highly Effective People*, both of which sat in front of her.

Emily stared at them for a long moment. It had been a while since she'd had an opportunity to sit in a quiet room doing something other than work or paying bills. She'd tried to take up journaling when Henry was little, hoping to record the moments of his life, but that had been a big fail as she struggled to find time to shower, let alone leisurely record how smart and cute her son was.

Turning her mind back to the items before her, she opened the journal and slid the book out of her way. Today, she'd respond to the question that had been gnawing at her since meeting David: Do I feel like I'm fulfilling what I'm meant to in life? Looking at the blank page, she realized she needed a pen and fished in her bag, finally retrieving one. She dated the page, noted her question at the top, and began writing.

The answer isn't simple or straightforward. At work, no. That's an obvious one. I'm successful in my role, but I'm at the point where I don't know how much longer I can be stagnant. It's not good for my growth as a person or, obviously, within the company.

As a mom, I feel mixed. I try so hard, but the demands of motherhood are bigger than I ever imagined. I'm lucky to have Jason. He carries a lot of the parenting load, even with his full schedule as a financial planner, but I am still managing most of the house, which is never as clean or organized as I want it to be. Worst of all, my stress at work often carries home, and I find myself forcing calmness and happiness on the outside but inwardly fretting over a deadline or issue at work—and yet, at the same time, wondering why I should even care if my company doesn't care about me?

I'm realizing something, though. I can control one thing about my work: me. Not just doing my role really well or leading my team effectively, both of which I already do, but <u>leading myself</u>. I have total control over me. It's a freeing realization.

The promotion, though. Will that ever happen? Will I ever get recognized for my hard work? Will a woman ever rise the way men do at my company? Do I have what it takes to pave the way?

Emily looked up from her writing and checked her watch. 8:27. She'd become lost in journaling and hadn't gotten to the book. Tomorrow, she decided.

Just then, she spotted Mitchell arriving at work. Seeing him reminded her of David's advice—that she needed to educate the people around her about her new discretionary time. She gave him fifteen minutes to settle in, checking her email as she waited, and then walked the short distance to his office.

She tapped on his open door. "Mitchell?"

"Morning." Mitchell had been typing but stopped, hands still on his keyboard.

"Have a minute?"

"Sure. What's going on?"

"Well, I'm starting something new, beginning this morning actually, and I want to talk to you about it."

"OK. Should we schedule time to talk?"

"No, no. I just want to share with you really quick." She walked into his office and stood in front of his desk. "I realized I haven't had enough space for personal development and thought. I come into work and I'm right at it, answering emails, running meetings—my day kicks into high gear from the moment I sit down."

"Sounds familiar." His brow was clenched, and Emily worried he might be misunderstanding her.

"Which I like. The momentum is good. But I've realized that space for personal development will never be made available for me, and if I want to grow, I need to make the time for myself."

"What do you mean?"

"Well, you may notice me coming in early a few days a week, maybe every day, and that's to create that space."

Mitchell's face relaxed. "That's great. We could certainly use the extra time around here."

Emily paused, remembering David's warning. "I want to be clear—I'm creating that space for my own growth and strategic thinking. I'm making discretionary time. Consider me here but not here."

Mitchell's brow drew inward again, and he stared at Emily as if considering her idea. "Here but not here?"

"Here but not here."

"What will you be doing?"

"It depends on the day. Today, I wrote. Tomorrow, I'll read. Some days I might do online training. Other days, I might work on a quarterly strategic plan for our team."

He was nodding, a slight smile on his face. "I'm impressed."

Really? she thought. "Thank you. I think it'll be great, too. See you at ten o'clock for our team meeting?"

"See you then."

Emily walked back to her office, a grin threatening to spread its way across her face. She had just influenced her boss, at least in theory. The true test would be the next few weeks of her new discretionary time. But still, maybe David was on to something.

—

Emily stood on her tiptoes in line at Slow by Slow, hoping to catch sight of David, but she couldn't see over the wall to the tables above. The line was long this morning, and each person who ordered seemed enthralled by the concept of slow coffee. She got it—pour-over was cool. And it was a Friday, so people were already on weekend time. But the average order time was nearing three minutes (not that she'd timed it or anything), and there were six people ahead of her. Maybe it will pick up speed, she thought. Please, let it pick up speed.

As Emily waited, she reflected on the past two weeks. They had been the best workweeks she'd had in a while, despite the stomach flu Henry had developed mid-week last week. She smiled to herself, thinking of Jason. He'd taken off half of the week to stay with Henry, bring him to the doctor, and generally hold life together.

The start of her new schedule was the week Henry had been sick, and she'd gotten in her thirty minutes of discretionary time Monday and Tuesday. With the flu onset on Wednesday, and needing to give Jason a parenting break Thursday and Friday morning, leaving early for work wasn't possible. This week, she'd managed four days; today was a skip day so she could stop by the coffee shop to hopefully see David. She wasn't acing David's assignment, but still, she felt good. Things were starting to shift.

Emily realized it was almost her turn at the coffee counter. She placed her order and hurried upstairs to find David. Sure enough, he sat at the same back corner table reading his tablet, a pastry sitting untouched on a plate in front of him and a newspaper to his left.

"Morning, David," Emily said, careful not to startle him.

"Good morning! I was hoping to see you." David stood and greeted her with a wide smile. "Actually, I've been hoping to see you for about two weeks now."

"I came looking for you. I want to tell you about my assignment. Plus, I felt like you could have kept talking for ten hours and still barely scratched the surface of what you know about leadership and influence."

David laughed. "I only know what I've learned over a lifetime of study and practice."

"Exactly." She paused for a beat before adding, "So, can we resume our lessons?"

David set down his tablet. "Only if you promise to teach me too. I still have a lot to learn."

"Deal."

At David's request, Emily filled him in on the two weeks that had passed since they'd last talked: the sick toddler, the conversation with her boss, her new discretionary time.

"Sounds like a productive couple of weeks. How about your virtuous conspiracy?"

"Oh, yes. That's under way."

Emily reported that they had their first celebratory lunch on the calendar. Right after she'd talked with David, she'd spent several days gathering a committee of five, herself included. She'd even gone to

Mitchell to get a $200 monthly budget for lunch and a gift—small, she knew, but it wasn't the amount that mattered. They would have just enough to present $25 gift cards to two honorees and host a monthly off-site pizza lunch.

"We developed a nomination process and tracking spreadsheet and everything," Emily said. "We're excited to present the first cards. And the best part? Our group is anonymous, and at this point, no one outside our group and my boss knows it exists. I think it's more fun that way. And it takes the focus off of our group and onto the person we're celebrating."

David's expression had shifted from intrigued interest to admiration. "You really took my advice to a different level. Nicely done."

"Thanks. It's been fun." Her eyes widened in surprise. "Wow, 'fun.' That's something I didn't expect to say about work."

"Nice change, isn't it?"

"It is." Emily paused for a moment. "You know, to be honest, following your advice has taken a lot of effort. Coming in early means going to bed early. Jason and I have such limited time in the evening that I wasn't sure if I could, or wanted to, give that time up. And thirty minutes early every day felt ambitious. I didn't know if I had it in me."

"And has it been worth it?"

"You know, I'm still not sure, but I think so. On the days that I come in early, I've noticed I'm able to leave earlier, and I'm getting more time with my family. I start the day with an organized brain, which makes me more productive. And I've used that time to complete tasks that require uninterrupted focus."

"Over time, I think you'll see the benefits amplify."

"I hope so. I only made it six out of ten days. Our son, Henry, got sick the first week, which made it tough."

"The point is to take ownership of what you have 100 percent control over. You can't control everything 100 percent when you have kids."

"Still, I think I was using Henry as an excuse."

"Meaning?"

"I was so used to having a baby as a reason for being tired, stressed, or whatever. I actually have more control than I realized." Emily looked at her hands for several seconds before meeting David's eyes. "Basically, I've met the enemy, and the enemy is me. No one was keeping me from having influence; it was always available to me."

David chuckled. "You sound like me at your age."

"Really?"

"Oh yeah. Did I mention that I have five kids?"

Emily stared at him. Her mouth dropped. Five kids?

"I see that surprises you."

Emily nodded. "More like impresses me."

"I understand how tough it can be to balance parenting and career."

"No kidding."

"Now, how about concern, the area where your influence is invisible right now?"

Emily admitted that she hadn't paid as much attention to the acquisition, but nothing had changed. "I've been focusing mostly on control and collaboration, which has shifted my energy away from the potential acquisition. The thing is, I still feel powerless in other areas."

"In what way?"

"I just wish there was more integrity in the way leadership treats me."

"How so?"

Emily stared at the table, then back up at David. "Little things. Yesterday, my boss, Mitchell, called me into a meeting that was already in progress. There were no chairs available, so I just stood there, feeling . . . I don't know. Small. And a few days before that, I heard him invite everyone in the room to get a drink after work. Except me. I just don't get it. I could go on, but I think you get the idea."

David thought for a moment. "Do you think he's not including you intentionally?"

"I don't, that's the thing. If I were to bring those instances up, I doubt he'd even remember."

"You said you wish leadership would treat you with more integrity. Let me ask you this question: What is integrity?" Before Emily could answer, David added, "Think about it for a moment. I'll be back."

Emily watched David walk to the back of the coffee shop toward the hall where the restrooms were. As she considered his question, she twisted in her chair, looking around the room. Everywhere she turned, it seemed there was another late-twenty-something working away on a computer. They were dressed much more stylishly than she was, and all but two were wearing big headphones—a trend Emily could never quite get behind. She thought of her earplugs safely tucked in her bag. Silence was her music.

As Emily watched frenetic fingers hacking away on keyboards, she wondered if these kids were working or on social media. She inwardly grinned at the idea that, at just thirty herself, she saw a twenty-something as a kid.

Ah, parenting, she thought. It really has aged me, hasn't it?

Her own twenties had been mostly work and little play—all focused on The Big Goal of climbing the corporate ladder. She'd missed out on having a real college experience. While her friends were out partying and dating, she'd been working full time, completing a part-time internship, and taking nearly a double load of credits. When she'd been hired at Enertec, it felt like her hard work had paid off. Now she wasn't so sure. Yes, she was starting to have fun in her work, but that wasn't enough. She felt stagnant. And yet, thanks to these meetings with David and the changes she was making because of them, she felt hopeful.

David returned and she spun back around, realizing she hadn't thought about his question at all.

"Well?" he asked. "Any thoughts on integrity?"

"I got a little distracted," Emily admitted. "But let's see. I guess I think of integrity as being honest and ethical. Not being duplicitous."

"That's a good start. But can I add to it?"

Emily nodded. "Please."

David grabbed his tablet, opened the browser, and typed a short phrase into the search. She watched his eyes scan the screen. Finally, he selected an image and turned the tablet around so Emily could view what he'd pulled up.

She was surprised to see an outline of the human body. Within the body was an intricate map of nerves connecting to the spinal cord, which connected to the brain. Underneath the image were the words *Nervous System*.

"In the human body, integrity of the nervous system refers to all the parts working and relating properly to each other," David said. "When all the parts properly interact—the neurons, spinal cord, and brain work in concert, sending and receiving messages—it results in a capacity that is greater than the sum of its parts. If they don't work together, it can lead to big problems." David set his tablet on the table in front of him, facing Emily. "Can you see how that could apply at work and with your senior leaders?"

Emily stared at the screen, trying to connect what he was saying. "To be honest, not really. I mean, I get the definition. It makes sense, and it's much more poetic than the one I offered. But I'm not sure I see the application."

"That's OK. Let's think about a team—a team is made up of several members and has a goal or objective it's trying to accomplish. And oftentimes, it's the relationship between the members that determines the success of the team, not just the individual capacities of the members. So, in a way, you could think of a well-functioning nervous system as a metaphor for how you'd want your team to function." He turned the tablet toward him and pushed a button at the top to darken the screen. "By the way, you have a team. Would you say the members function synergistically, with a capacity greater than the sum of its parts?"

Emily shook her head. "That's a definite no. But your explanation makes a lot of sense. I get how it applies to my work now."

"Great." He pointed to Emily's watch. "How are you on time?"

"I've got to run in about fifteen minutes."

"All right, so with that in mind, I'd like to shift our discussion to talk more about influence."

"Perfect."

"We discussed influence through what you can control, where you can collaborate, and where you have concerns—and that last one is admittedly the most distant and often invisible. But I'd like to propose to you that a leader is a person of influence."

"You know, we were just talking about leadership in the professional group I attend." David listened in interest as Emily went on. "Did I tell you about that? It's a women's group that meets every month to talk about an aspect of leadership. We grow together. Before our last meeting, we read *The Effective Executive*. In it, Peter Drucker says, 'The only thing you can say about a leader is that a leader is somebody who has followers.'"

"Your group sounds great, and I'm a big fan of Drucker, but I think that definition is fairly narrow," David said.

There's that directness, Emily thought. "What do you mean?"

"Well, actually I think there may be a broader, more aspirational definition of a leader—that a leader is a person of influence who has learned to work properly within the three areas of influence."

Emily had opened up the notes app on her phone and was typing. She looked at David. "Can you say that again?"

"A leader is a person of influence who has learned to work properly within the three areas of influence."

Emily looked up from typing. "Within control, collaboration, and concern?"

"Right."

"Interesting. So, a leader can be anyone, not just someone with the title of president, VP, or something like that."

"Absolutely. In fact, I bet you know people in your company who have a lot of influence and don't have a title."

Emily thought for a moment. One person came to mind quickly. "Karen. My boss's executive assistant. She practically runs our department."

"Good example. Why is that? What is it about Karen that gives her so much influence?"

"Well, she gets things done. If I need something, I almost always go to her first because I know she'll help me. Plus, she's kind—she treats me with respect. I want to make her happy. And keep her happy," Emily added with a laugh.

"Great point. You definitely want to keep people like Karen happy. It sounds like you see her as an informal leader, is that right?"

"I guess I do. If a leader is a person of influence, then I'd have to say she's a leader. I can think of a few people who are informal leaders in our company."

"That sounds like something we ought to talk about next time we run into each other."

At this, Emily sat forward a little. Her hands started sweating, and her heart raced a bit. She'd been wanting to ask David something since the last time they met.

"Maybe we can also talk about a broader definition of integrity in the context of leadership," he continued. "In fact, there are three dimensions."

"Another set of three?"

"Yes. And maybe the most important concept I can share with you, the three dimensions of leadership."

"Three dimensions," Emily echoed. She grew quiet, trying to slow her quickening breath. She was eager to learn from him, to improve and grow, but how could she be sure there would be a next time? Was he as interested in continuing their conversations as she was, or was he merely being polite? Maybe she'd intruded too much upon his time already.

"You know . . ." she began, taking a breath. She paused. Did she really want to ask this of someone who'd already given her so much and so freely?

"Yes?"

"Well, our conversations have stayed with me. I'm wondering, would you be willing to get together every now and then and continue to share your knowledge and experience with me?" Emily looked at the table and then met David's eyes. "I have a feeling you might know more than you've revealed to me so far." She paused, searching for just the right words. "But I don't want to overstep or disrupt your peaceful mornings, so if—"

David put up a hand. "I'd love to."

"Really?"

"Yes. And I'm certain I can learn from you as well."

Emily doubted she had much to teach, but a quick glance to her watch stopped her thoughts.

"I've got to go. Do you want to set something up now?" David nodded as Emily opened the calendar on her phone. "How about next Saturday?"

"I don't normally come in on Saturdays, but I'm sure my wife won't mind."

"Oh, no. Let's do a more convenient day for you."

"Next Saturday works great."

"You sure?"

"How about nine o'clock?"

"That's perfect." Emily stood, slung her bag over her shoulder, and looked David straight in the eyes. "Thank you, David. This means a lot to me."

"It does to me too."

After saying goodbye, Emily walked through the coffee shop and out the door. As she undid the lock on her bicycle, she thought through their conversation. She felt hopeful, like there was something big on the horizon. For the first time, it was like she was beginning to develop a map of her life, a way to overcome the obstacles that were holding her back in her career. Just a few weeks ago, her only solution was to finally get a promotion, but a bigger title and more responsibility didn't feel as important anymore. Discretionary time, the virtuous conspiracy, and shifting her attention away from the acquisition were great starts, but she knew there was more David could offer her.

What's different? she wondered. What's shifted inside of me?

Then it hit her: I've always had drive; I've never had purpose.

As she buckled her helmet, she decided who her celebration group would be honoring first: Karen. Emily pedaled away, thinking about what she'd write in Karen's card—anonymously, of course. When the group had met, they'd started a list of people who achieved tangible results, who were making things happen. Just one conversation with David had shifted her view of what "tangible results" and "making things happen" meant. Now, they'd seek out not just the people who launched successful products or won big contracts but also people who were contributing in less glamorous ways. The everyday heroes of the company. People who kept things running smoothly. People who made her work easier. People like Karen.

Minutes later, she arrived at work, locked her bike, and looked up at the tall building. The sense of dread she'd been feeling for months had disappeared, and in its place was a faint glimmer of promise, even excitement. She had always wanted to feel this way at work. True, Mitchell was still there, as was the general patriarchal overlay, but she knew that didn't mean she was doomed to a life of missed opportunities. She could gain greater influence.

Emily opened the door and made her way into the building, looking around at the modern lobby with its royal blue wingback chairs, distressed wood floors, and expensive abstract art. She pushed the elevator button, stepped in and selected the third floor, and rode the seconds-long lift to her workplace.

Today is the day, she thought. It's finally time to ask Mitchell why I keep getting passed over for promotions.

—

2:55. Emily was staring at the clock on her computer, willing herself to stay calm.

She still hadn't talked to Mitchell about the promotion. She'd attempted several times, but each instance when she made her way to his door, someone was in there. Finally, she messaged him and asked if he could talk at 3:00. He replied that he had 15 minutes.

Even better, Emily had thought, no need to drag this out.

When the clock rolled around to 2:58, Emily stood, smoothed her hair, retucked the front of her shirt, and walked toward her office door. With a moment's hesitation, she opened it and crossed the short distance to Mitchell's office. When she arrived, the door was slightly ajar, so she lightly knocked.

"Emily?" Mitchell called. "Come in. Let me just finish this email before we get started."

Emily closed the door behind her and sat in one of the two chairs in front of Mitchell's desk. For several minutes, the only sound was the clackety-clack of the keyboard as he pounded out an email. She watched his fingers, nervousness growing as she waited. Finally, the room grew silent as he sat up, folded his hands, and reread his message. She saw him reach for his mouse and click. Sent.

Mitchell turned his attention to Emily. "Sorry about that. Fires. Gotta put them out."

Emily nodded. "Yep, I get that."

"So, what's up?"

"Thanks for making time today," Emily began. She hesitated, unsure of how to begin even though she'd run it through her head dozens of times. "I have something I'd like to ask you."

"What is it?"

"You know a few weeks ago when you told me about Stan's promotion?" Mitchell just nodded, so Emily went on. "I've been going over and over in my mind about why he was promoted over me. And it's not the first time I've been passed up. A lot of my colleagues are getting promoted, and I feel like I'm at a standstill." She scanned his face, but his expression was unreadable, so she pressed on. "To be honest, Mitchell, I work harder than they do. If you look at the monthly reports, I nearly always come out measurably better. They're great people and good at what they do, I'm not saying they aren't, but I'm having a hard time understanding what they have that I don't."

Mitchell looked at her thoughtfully for several seconds as Emily forced herself to sit tall and confident. Finally, he stood, walked around his desk, and sat in the chair next to her. She turned to face him.

"Look, Emily, no one appreciates you more than I do. You're a superstar. You're committed, trustworthy, respected, and you come through every time. No question." He paused, as if forming the words in his head. "But can I be straight with you?"

"Please."

"It's nothing about your performance. You get ten out of ten in nearly every aspect of your work and management."

"Then what is it?"

Now Mitchell was the one who looked uncomfortable. "Look, I don't know how to put this. I guess I haven't felt that it was . . . well, appropriate to ask you to take on more responsibility."

Emily blinked. "Appropriate?"

"Right. Because you have so much going on at home, being a mom, I mean. I didn't want to put more pressure on you."

"It's because I'm a mom?"

"No, no, no. Not because you're a mom. I just wanted to be sensitive, Emily. I'm looking out for you." Mitchell smiled and patted her on the shoulder.

It took everything in Emily not to recoil from his touch as the dull feeling of anger crowded out the nervousness she'd felt walking into that room. She looked at Mitchell. She hadn't noticed how much he'd aged since she'd started there. His blond hair was thinning, he'd grown a slight belly, and wrinkles had crept around his eyes. It struck her suddenly that Mitchell had been in the same position for nearly a decade. He'd never married, never had kids. This job was his whole life. To him, having responsibilities outside of work—having a life—made her less effective. Kids were a professional liability.

But then again, some of her male colleagues had kids, and they were still getting promotions.

"Mitchell," she said, steadying her voice, "I know you think you're looking out for me, but all you're doing is holding me back." Mitchell's eyes grew wide, and he sat up in his chair, ready to speak, but Emily went on. "What about Stan? He has two kids. And James? He was promoted a year ago, and his baby was only three months old. And how about Cameron? He has a kid!" Emily's anger was slipping out, so she stopped talking but kept her gaze firmly on Mitchell.

Mitchell was staring at her. He shifted in his seat and tapped his fingers quickly against the arm of the chair. Emily had never seen him so uncomfortable. "They all deserved those promotions," he finally said, his voice low. "And they weren't the primary caregivers at home. They are all in."

"I have just as much help at home as they do. And I work harder than every one of those men." There, she'd said it. Men.

"But you're torn between home and here. I need you here."

"So, what can I do, Mitchell? How can I ever advance in this company? I'm not going to abandon my kid."

Mitchell looked at her carefully. "I'm not asking you to. But I need to count on you to put work first."

"You mean before my son."

"I didn't say that," Mitchell replied, his voice softening. "Look, just consider what I said. I think you'll start to see I'm right."

Emily swallowed. It was the only strategy she'd mastered to keep her anger from spewing out at the wrong times. She was grateful now for the decade of mindfulness training she'd worked at so diligently—all for moments like this, when she wanted to explode.

"I don't think I will, Mitchell," she finally said.

He forced a smile. "I just want you to succeed."

Emily stood, righted her chair, and left Mitchell's office without another word. She sat at her own desk and stared at the opposite wall for nearly ten minutes, her mind running through the discussion. She breathed in for five seconds, out for five. In, out. Her body relaxed.

Then, Emily turned toward the right side of her desk, where her red work bag was sitting on the floor. In it was a brown paper bag, the contents of which she'd picked up on her lunch break. She opened the bag and peered inside. There sat an unopened box, small and yet looming. On the front in flowing type were the words: *Pregnancy Test.*

$$\text{4}$$

For Now, Ignore Position

Emily had hardly slept since her discussion with Mitchell the previous week and had already been up for two hours that Saturday morning. Why not head in early to meet David? Jason and Henry were having a leisurely breakfast at home, and she knew they'd enjoy the solo time together.

As she pedaled past newly built buildings in downtown Boise, she thought back on her week. Mitchell had been avoiding her since their talk, and every time she'd spoken to one of the men who'd been promoted over her, she'd felt a deep uneasiness that didn't seem to go away. Mitchell's face flashed in her mind, the patronizing expression he'd worn when he'd explained that motherhood was the reason she wasn't getting promoted. She tightened her grip on the handlebars. Didn't he realize he was engaging in blatant discrimination? And then there was the pregnancy test.

Emily shook her head abruptly, willing the scene—Mitchell, the purple pregnancy box, the entire week—out of her mind. Suddenly, she knew what she needed. Instead of going straight to Slow by Slow, she made a U-turn and headed toward the Boise foothills.

Locking her bike at Camel's Back Park, Emily looked at the empty slides and swings. It was 8:10, and there was one lone person on the workout equipment just past the playground. As she removed her helmet and turned around, she spotted nearly two dozen runners and bikers setting out on their morning workouts. Her people.

Emily smiled to herself. She could use a run or mountain bike ride, too, but not today. This morning, she had a meeting with her new mentor, and before that, she needed peace and clarity.

Emily fast-walked to the base of Camel's Back hill and looked up. The park was aptly named for the steep slope shaped like a camel's hump that rose high above the park. As a kid, she'd spent entire afternoons climbing the steep hill and then running down the slick, sandy facade, often falling into the soft sand and rolling, rolling, rolling.

That morning, Emily opted for the less-sandy route to the top and took a windy side path. By the time she reached the summit, her breathing had deepened. The top was empty—a rarity on mornings like this. She climbed over to the old wooden fence toward the front of the hill and sat down on the rail, looking out at the sprawling cityscape. With closed eyes, she took the crispness of the morning into her lungs and exhaled the negativity that had plagued her all week.

She wasn't looking to forget. Nor to forgive—yet. But she knew that steadiness was going to be her best tool to change the patriarchy of Enertec. In order to gain influence, she had to lead herself first. In this moment, that meant steadying her emotions and calming her mind.

Emily peeked at her watch. Half an hour until her meetup with David. She sat there for three more long minutes, meditating on the morning, feeling exhalations on her lips, pushing images of Mitchell out of her mind and replacing them with Henry and Jason. Finally, she opened her eyes, stood, and climbed back over the gate. Walking to the edge of the hill, Emily peered down the steep slope of her childhood. Had it been fifteen years? Twenty? Finally, she descended a set of stone steps and placed her feet on the sandy slope. She took a few steps forward, and broke into a run.

Emily rushed down the hill, wind pushing back her hair, the adrenaline of grade school returning with every hurried step. She slipped and caught herself, then kept running, well past the base of the sand, across the park, and to the playground. She stopped short of her bike and put her hands on her knees.

Her face was red and her lungs were burning, but elation had spread the length of her body. She stood, hands interlaced on the top of her head, lifting her face to the sun. Her body felt light. Open. Her mind, calm and certain. Her anger, far away—like she'd left it at the top of the hill.

Better, she thought. Now I'm ready for David.

—

Fifteen minutes later, Emily sat at one of the two-person tables at Slow by Slow. The place was packed, and David's regular table hadn't been available. When the barista brought her coffee, she checked her watch. 9:08.

It didn't seem like David to be late—but then, what did she really know about him? This was only the fourth time they'd met, and the first time had been a mess of coffee and wet napkins, so that didn't really count. Still, it seemed odd. She would have pegged David as the punctual type, the kind of guy who arrives ten minutes early everywhere he goes.

"Emily," David said, snapping Emily out of her thoughts. "I'm late. I apologize."

"Good morning!" Emily said, surprised at her enthusiasm. She rose to shake his hand. "I wondered if you were going to stand me up."

"Never. I had an interesting morning. But I'm here now."

"Want some coffee?"

"I already ordered. Thanks."

Emily sat and watched as David settled into his chair. His face was flushed—from rushing to the coffee shop, she assumed—and there were faint gray rings under his eyes, like he'd had a rough night's sleep.

He looked squarely at Emily. "Shall we?"

Emily chuckled. "You're all business."

"Well, I'm here for you today. And I promised my wife I'd meet her at the farmer's market at 10:15, so we'd better jump in." Emily nodded as David continued. "Remember last time how we talked about influencers? You identified informal influencers in your organization—people without titles but with influence."

"Like Karen, the executive assistant. Our group is celebrating her next week."

"That's excellent. It sounds like she deserves it."

"She really does."

"Will you humor me for a minute while I ask you some questions about Karen and other influencers in your company?" David asked.

"Sure," Emily replied. She watched him dig into a distressed leather satchel and pull out a notepad and pen.

David noticed her staring at his bag. "My wife. It's vegan leather—definitely not something I would have picked out."

Emily lifted her eyebrows. "She has good taste."

David set the notepad on the desk. It was a blank pad—no lines or grids. Emily realized that he must have packed it just for their discussion. He removed the pen cap and drew three columns.

"First, why is Karen influential in your company?"

She considered his question. "She gets things done. She's kind, respectful, and always follows through." Emily watched as David wrote *gets things done, kind, respectful,* and *follows through* in the third column.

"What else? What gives other people in your organization influence?"

"I suppose being knowledgeable about how things work."

David wrote *knowledgeable* in the middle column. "Keep going. What are other qualities of influencers in your organization?"

"The engineers are respected for their intelligence. And they're really good at problem solving." Emily watched David write *smart* and *problem solving* in the middle column before she went on. "I just thought of one person who took an interest in me when I was a new manager trainee. We'd go to lunch once a month and talk about my growth in the company—where I was heading. He'd share stories about his experience moving from being an engineer to becoming a leader within the organization."

"Good example," David said. "How would you describe him? What trait was influential?"

"Hmm. Maybe helpful."

David wrote *helpful* in the third column. "How was he helpful?"

"Well, he was generous with his time. And like Karen, he was knowledgeable about how things work at our company." As David wrote *generous* in the third column, Emily added, "And he's an expert engineer, which I really admire. He's also highly accomplished." David added *expert* and *accomplished* to the second column.

"Good. Now, I haven't heard you say anything yet about people who are influential because of their job titles. Who comes to mind when I say that?"

"The CEO, of course," Emily said, pausing as David wrote *CEO* in the first column. "And the senior VP of research has a big voice because he's been key to the success of the company, maybe even more than the CEO." David wrote *senior VP* in the first column.

"Any others?"

Emily looked at her coffee, rolling the mug between her hands slowly clockwise, then counterclockwise. "I suppose it depends on what your role is in the company. Mitchell influences my life and the lives of my colleagues because he makes decisions about our future."

"Is he a director?" David said. When Emily nodded, he wrote *director* in the first column, then spun the paper around so Emily could read it.

CEO Senior VP Director	Knowledgeable Smart Problem Solving Expert Accomplished	Gets Things Done Kind Respectful Follows Through Helpful Generous

Emily surveyed the paper in front of her. "Interesting. There are just titles in the first column but descriptors in the other two columns." She looked up at David. "I'm guessing you're going to explain the meaning?"

David nodded and pointed to the paper with his pen. "What you've done is help me map out three dimensions of leadership in your organization." He rotated the paper back around and wrote titles above each of the columns, then turned it again to Emily.

"Positional leadership, expert leadership, character leadership," Emily read.

"Exactly. We'll call this first dimension positional leadership, or you could also call it structural leadership. It's the influence people have because of their title." He tapped the middle list with his pen. "This second column is expert leadership, which is the influence people have in the organization because of what they know or have accomplished. And this third column with the most descriptors is character leadership. It's the influence people have because of who they are. The core idea of the three dimensions of leadership is that influence *is* leadership, and a leader's true influence is some combination of all three dimensions. Each of these dimensions of leadership has separate measures of integrity."

POSITIONAL LEADERSHIP	EXPERT LEADERSHIP	CHARACTER LEADERSHIP
CEO	KNOWLEDGEABLE	GETS THINGS DONE
SENIOR VP	SMART	KIND
DIRECTOR	PROBLEM SOLVING	RESPECTFUL
	EXPERT	FOLLOWS THROUGH
	ACCOMPLISHED	HELPFUL
		GENEROUS

Emily stared at the paper. All this time, she had been aspiring to reach a position. She'd struggled her entire career to reach the next and better title, the bigger paycheck, more responsibilities, inclusion with the executive team. But when defining influence in her organization, clearly expertise and character were what mattered. She may not have even thought of positional leaders without David's prompting. Knowledgeable, problem-solving, helpful, respectful, generous—these were all things she wanted to be. She'd always considered a title necessary to have influence in her company, but really, anyone could have influence.

And then there was Mitchell. He was a positional leader, but to what end? He lacked expert and character leadership. At this stage in her career, Emily considered herself more of an expert than Mitchell even though he was her boss, and she certainly had more character. Passing her over for a promotion because she's a mother surely didn't fit into the character column.

"Emily?" David said, his voice quiet. "Looks like you have a lot going on in that head of yours."

She looked up. Her breath was shallow. She felt anger swelling in her chest, the same anger she'd worked so hard to release earlier that morning.

"I'm just—" Emily stopped herself, not sure how much she should go into her week. This discussion was about growth, not stagnation.

"Did I say something to upset you?" David asked.

"No, no. Not at all," Emily replied. "I had a frustrating discussion with my boss last week. I've been trying to just be present this morning, but all this talk about integrity is bringing back what happened."

"What are you feeling right now?"

Emily hesitated, her eyes on the list. She looked at David. "I'm OK. Let's keep going. I want to learn."

"We can take a detour. I promise we'll get back to it."

She looked at David, considering whether to share. Finally, she spoke. "I'm angry."

"Why are you angry?"

Emily recapped the entire discussion with Mitchell—how she'd finally gotten up the courage to talk to him about why he'd passed her up for the promotion, how he'd used motherhood as his reason for holding her back. After several minutes of retelling, Emily was quiet.

Finally, she said, "I just don't know how I'm ever going to reach my potential in a place where I'm not treated equally."

David looked her directly in the eyes. "I don't think I'll ever fully understand what you're dealing with right now. I'm sorry you're going through it." David shook his head, looking at the ceiling as though processing her hurt. "Have you thought about looking for a position at another company?"

"Yes. But I don't see much point. From talking with friends in other companies, both here and across the US, I'm convinced this is the way it is in corporate America right now. Or at least in the technology field. And I've also thought about reporting him, but the issue is so pervasive, I don't think it'll accomplish anything, other than maybe ostracizing me from the local tech community. I think the only option is to try to influence him."

David nodded. "How is this impacting you personally?"

"It's just . . . it's crushing. I don't know a better way to describe it. I'm not sure how loyal I can be to this company." Emily was surprised to hear herself say this out loud. She prided herself in evenness, in an ability to take things as they came, even hard things. But this—this was different. It was a powerlessness she'd never felt before.

A respectful pause stretched between them before David spoke. "When I try to understand your experience, I realize how silly it is to think I can ever grasp the fullness of it."

Emily offered a half smile. "Having this conversation is at least a step toward understanding." She considered her words before continuing. "The thing is, the media reports on men who discriminate against women, and do other harmful things, knowing full well what they're doing. But almost every day, I hear something, read something, see something, or experience something that's not intentional."

David let out a low whistle, as though someone had knocked air out of his chest. "I had no idea the issue is that pervasive."

"It is. Nearly every woman I know has a story like mine . . . or worse. At least Mitchell hasn't sexually harassed me. Believe me, there are plenty of women who have confided in me about terrible experiences with their bosses." Emily realized she was looking past David, at the door to the back hall, and shifted her gaze to meet his. When he said nothing, she asked, "Any advice?"

David screwed his mouth to one side, thinking. "Well," he said, letting a long pause hang in the air, "I don't feel qualified to speak to the discrimination you're facing, but can I offer advice I've shared with other young women and men over the years?"

"Please."

"For now, let's ignore the position so you can get the position."

Emily blinked. "What?"

"Ignore the position so you can get the position."

"I heard you. But what does that mean?"

"Unfortunately, I don't have time to explain. I have a very patient wife waiting for me at the farmer's market." At this, David winked. "Next week?"

"What? You can't do this to me." She was smiling, her anger nearly forgotten.

"I'm sorry, but I made a commitment to my wife. When are you available next week? I'm here every weekday morning."

Emily mock-groaned and pulled up the calendar on her phone. "I'll move a meeting so I can make it on Thursday. But wait, what should I tell Mitchell? I'm not sure I can make it that long without addressing what happened."

"The time will come when you can speak with power," David said.
"And until then?"

"We'll get to that soon. Maximum power is often a matter of timing. If you don't pick the right time, you won't get the results you're looking for. There will be a right time for you to speak to your boss with clarity, but it's important to figure out when that time is. It's not just about knowing what to say; it's understanding when to say it."

"I've never thought of it that way."

"Neither had I until I learned it the hard way." Emily blinked quickly, startled. Not until that moment had she thought of David learning his way through leadership just like she was, struggling through missed opportunities and disappointments. He'd been on her side of the table, learning these same lessons.

"If something comes up between now and Thursday, lead with logic, follow with emotion," he added. "That's the best advice I can give you."

"Lead with logic, follow with emotion. Something tells me you just said something significant."

David stood and pushed in his chair, a gleam in his eyes. "We'll see, won't we?"

"I guess we will," Emily said, then pointed to her watch. "You'd better get going."

"You're right." David placed his pad and pen in his bag. "Can I give you some homework this week?"

"Please."

"I'd like you to think and journal about how you might define integrity in the dimension of character leadership."

"On it."

"See you soon."

"Thanks, David." Emily stood and reached out to shake David's hand. He smiled and opened his arms for a hug. They embraced, and David walked toward the stairs to leave.

"Oh, and David?" Emily called over the noisy shop.

"Yes?" he said, turning to face her.

"I've been meaning to tell you—I'm pregnant."

Character First

Emily twirled her pen, watching it spin once, twice, before catching it between her thumb and index finger. She looked out the window at the long shadows cast by thickly crowned trees. Their shade looked like bellies to her—big, pregnant bellies. But then again, everything reminded her of the baby.

Jason was ecstatic. And she was too, except for the gnawing feeling that having this baby meant another stall in her career of at least a year or two. If Mitchell thought she was overextended *now*, what would he think when this child was born?

And it wasn't just Mitchell. She'd overheard a comment by one of her coworkers the other day, a single guy who worked in a different department. "She just left for her maternity vacation," he'd said to another male colleague, laughing. "Don't you wish we could do that? And then come back and work basically part time?"

Emily hadn't said anything. Everything in her body had screamed at her to set him straight, but she hadn't. She had been too busy thinking of herself and what he'd say when she went on maternity leave.

To be fair, there were other parents and a handful of single women in her organization who vocally supported maternity and paternity leave. One of the two women in executive leadership roles had even left a major meeting to care for a sick child. Her decision had caused a rumble of general disapproval about "priorities" not just in Enertec but throughout the industry. Still, it was encouraging that she'd left the meeting, regardless of the backlash.

Emily was grateful to have a few allies, but that wouldn't be enough—there needed to be a cultural shift, and the only way she saw that happening was by starting with herself and her team. Telling off an insensitive coworker in the hallway wasn't what she needed to do. She needed to gain influence.

Emily checked her watch. 5:30. She rolled her chair back and stood, then sat and rolled back toward her desk. Jason wouldn't be home with Henry until 6:15, so why head home now? The office was quiet—most of her coworkers had cleared out early—and she still had the assignment from David. She had been pondering his question all week and wanted to write some thoughts down before they met the next morning.

Emily reached into her bag for her journal and a pen. She tapped her keyboard to wake her computer from sleep mode, pulled up a browser, and typed in the word "integrity." One definition caught Emily's eye, so she wrote down "the quality or state of being complete or undivided."[1] David had asked her to think about integrity in the dimension of character leadership. She wrote in her journal:

---

1   "Integrity." *Merriam-webster.com.*

I see integrity in character leadership as staying connected to my values, even in frustrating, challenging, or difficult situations. To me, character leaders are people I respect because of the way they treat other people, stay true to their word, and live ethically. They often have strong convictions, but they don't express them as divisive opinions-as-facts. They listen well. They lead respectfully. They are transparent. They live in a "quality or state of being complete or undivided" because they remain connected to their core—to their values.

This is the type of leader I want to be. I want to be influential because I'm living fully and completely in alignment with my heart. I want people to trust me because I am honest and truthful. I want them to feel heard, like someone is really looking at them and listening to what they have to say. In that way, I suppose, a character leader is fully present. Character leadership, I think, requires a certain vulnerability that expert and positional leadership do not.

One thing I'm struggling with, though, is how the three dimensions of leadership interact. I know position matters. So does expertise. But how much? Do I put most of my attention into character? How much do I focus on expertise? If I put all my energy into character and expertise, will I ever grow my position in the company? I'm looking forward to getting answers to these questions during my discussions with David.

Emily dated the top of the page and placed the journal in her bag. She had two handsome boys to get home to.

—

The next morning, Emily arrived at Slow by Slow twenty minutes early. She wanted to read before David arrived. After ordering her coffee, she made her way to the long table at the back of the shop and sat near the wall, facing the stairs.

Emily reached into her bag, pulled out *Lean In,* a book on women in leadership she'd purchased years ago but had just recently started reading, and opened up to her bookmark. She scanned the page to find the spot where she'd left off.

"It is impossible to control all the variables when it comes to parenting," it read. "For women who have achieved previous success by planning ahead and pushing themselves hard, this chaos can be difficult to accept."[2]

This wasn't exactly the rallying cry Emily had been hoping for, but at least it was real. She read on as Sandberg detailed her first maternity leave, during which she was constantly working from home, barely enjoying her new baby, and then her second leave, when she actually unplugged and enjoyed her children.

"Slowly, it began to dawn on me that my job did not really require I spend twelve full hours a day in the office," Sandberg wrote. "I became much more efficient—more vigilant about only attending or setting up meetings that were truly necessary, more

---

2   Sheryl Sandberg, *Lean In* (New York: Knopf, 2013), 125, 129.

determined to maximize my output during every minute I spent away from home. . . . I tried to focus on what really mattered." Sandberg essentially ran a company, and even she was able to find a way to be present at home and at work.

By 9:00, the time Emily was expecting David, she was feeling much better—inspired, even. She closed her book and watched the stairway, excited for their discussion. At 9:05, he emerged with a smile and a wave. Emily stood.

"David! So glad to see you," she said.

"Glad to see you, too, Emily." He had a to-go cup in his hand. "Shall we walk today?"

"Sounds nice. Let me get this to go." Emily gathered her book and bag. As they walked toward the door, she noticed he was moving slower than normal, and the bags under his eyes were still there.

"Everything OK?"

"Oh, yes," he said. "Just a little tired."

"You sure?"

David waved her concern away. "No, no. I'm fine. And anyway, I should be asking you that. How are you feeling?"

"A little nauseous, but good." She tapped her coffee mug. "Cutting caffeine has been hard. Decaf just isn't the same."

"Need a refill?" the barista asked Emily as they approached the counter.

"Just a warm-up. Decaf. And can you make it to go?"

"Yep."

David glanced at the book tucked under Emily's arm. "*Lean In*, huh? I enjoyed that book."

"You've read it?"

"Of course I have. You look surprised."

"A little, yeah." Emily dropped her bag to the ground and knelt to put her book inside. "I can't say I've met a man yet who has read it—let alone a retired CEO." She laughed. "You continue to astonish me."

The barista handed Emily her coffee and a cardboard sleeve. "This is hot."

"Got it. Thank you."

David nodded to the barista.

"Shall we?" Emily said to David, sliding the sleeve onto her cup.

"I was thinking we could walk toward the library and onto the greenbelt."

"Perfect. And then you'll tell me what you meant by 'ignore the position so you can get the position,' right?"

David laughed. "In due time. Now, I gave you an assignment last time," he said as they made their way outside. "Did you have time to complete it?"

"I did. I thought about it all week, and I spent some time writing about it last night. Would you like to read what I wrote?"

David nodded as Emily handed over her coffee, slid her bag from her shoulder, and retrieved her journal. She clutched it in her hands. "Before you read this, and we get into a whole discussion about integrity and whatnot, can I tell you what I learned this week?"

"Sure," David responded, handing back her coffee. "What's on your mind?"

The two stopped at an intersection and waited for the light to change. "Well, last time you talked about leading with logic and following with emotion. That's such a powerful concept, and I've started noticing that the people around me often do the opposite. All week long, as I've sat in meetings or talked with other leaders, I've asked myself, 'Which is in front, emotion or logic?' And I can't believe how revealing that is, just to ask that simple question."

"Was there a specific instance that stood out?"

"Yes, in one meeting with my peers." As they crossed the street and continued toward the greenbelt, Emily shared that she'd been in a meeting with other managers in the organization. They were talking about a new documentation platform senior leaders had asked them to use, replacing the software they'd built in the company's early days. Managers who had come through the trainee program were emotionally tied to the software they'd helped build, while newer hires were excited about the change. They'd spent nearly an hour discussing when and how to introduce the new platform to their teams and had gotten nowhere.

"You know when the frustration in a room is so thick you can almost feel it?" David nodded as Emily went on. "I began to notice that managers who had come through the trainee program with me were sending us into circular arguments, while the newer managers were growing frustrated and not staying focused on solutions, either. It became us versus them." She shook her head. "Normally, I might have been right in there, adding to the back and forth, but there I was, observing. I didn't say much the entire meeting. Finally, I suggested we regroup the next afternoon. I asked each manager to bring three things they'd like to see in the transition, and we'd work together to strategize. Everyone seemed glad to get out of there."

David was silent for several steps. They'd entered a quiet portion of Eighth Street. Instead of walking toward the greenbelt, he headed toward a bridge overlooking the river. He stopped when they reached the middle of the bridge and placed his forearms on the rail, looking out at the water. Emily stood next to him.

"You know," he began, "you're learning one of the most valuable lessons about how a leader uses emotional intelligence to influence others. Of course, there's a lot more to emotional intelligence than awareness and managing your own emotions; it's also being able to understand and work with other people's emotions. That's what you did in that meeting."

"I guess I did." She leaned against the rail, watching leaves and branches in the river below disappear under the bridge. "The real test will come in tomorrow's meeting."

"Right, but you should be proud of what you've accomplished so far. You're growing yourself as a leader, because the first step to leadership growth is self-awareness—a greater ability to stand back and recognize what's happening within you and around you. You stepped in and influenced a situation that was going nowhere."

Emily realized she was still holding her journal. "Well, I'm glad you think I'm growing, because I'm not sure I did what you wanted with the assignment of defining integrity in character leadership."

"What do you mean?" David asked.

"Well, I was able to define what I think integrity means for character. But I'm having a hard time understanding how all this fits together. I know the three dimensions of leadership—character, expert, positional—is the key thread, the main idea I need to keep anchoring back to. But I'm a little puzzled because you said there were three different definitions for integrity, and I don't know how it all connects."

"You're right. There are three dimensions of leadership. Each is important, and integrity within each is defined differently. Today we're going to talk about integrity in character leadership; we'll get to the others soon. Let's see what you wrote." She opened the journal to her most recent entry and handed it to him. He set his cup on the rail.

Emily couldn't help but study David's face as he read. He looked so—what was it? *Engaged.* Like he was reading the best book of his life.

Finally, he looked up. "This is great, Emily. Really thoughtful."

Emily smiled. "Thanks."

"You say, 'To me, character leaders are people I respect because of the way they treat other people, stay true to their word, and live ethically.' Later, you say, 'They live in a "quality or state of being complete or undivided" because they remain connected to their core—to their values.' This is insightful."

Emily's face flushed. She'd never heard her personal writing read aloud before. "Well, thank you. But to be honest, I'm not sure I could get specific about what that means, 'connected to their values.' I think that phrase is thrown around a lot, but when I really consider it, I don't know that I could even list my own values, and I certainly couldn't define the values of my boss or boss's boss."

"That's OK. For a long time, I felt the same way." He handed her journal back. "Want to keep walking?"

"Sure."

They continued along the length of the bridge, heading toward a curving path that would take them onto the greenbelt, which ran

Boise River. As they entered the greenbelt, they
ty coffee cups into a trash bin.

◡ι my coaches back in my CEO days challenged me to
think about character differently and broaden my definition of
integrity," David said. "And that quest led me to a book by Jim
Loehr called *The Only Way to Win.*"

Emily pulled her phone from her back pocket, opened her notes
app, and typed in the book title. "What was so profound about it
for you?"

"Reading it changed the way I thought about integrity in character leadership. As I applied what I learned in my own leadership,
I built on Loehr's ideas. I began to recognize that character can be
defined by how we answer two questions. The first question is, what
values will I choose to govern myself? And the second question is,
what values will I choose to relate to other people?"

Emily tilted her head in thought. "That is such a different way to
look at it. I typically think of values as a list of ways you want to live
your life, like honesty or loyalty. But you're saying to frame it as two
lists, one for myself and one for how I treat others. Tell me more."

"Let's think a little bit about what values you could choose to
govern yourself. Identifying values doesn't mean you're going to be
perfect—you're kind of creating your own leadership constitution,
defining the things that are most important to you. At the end of
your career, you want to be able to say, 'I governed myself according
to these things.'"

"Mind if we sit?" Emily said, motioning to a nearby bench looking out over the river. "I'd like to write some of this down."

"Good idea."

They settled in, and Emily opened her journal. She looked at her previous entry, then flipped to a new page and wrote *Values by which I choose to govern myself* at the top. "I guess I wrote about some of my values already," she said. "I want to be honest. I don't want to get to the end of my career and realize I've deceived others or been dishonest with myself."

"That's a great one. What are some other values you can think of?"

"Well, I want to be productive—get a lot done."

"OK. Maybe we could call that self-management?"

"Yeah, that's it."

"As a matter of fact, I have my own definition of self-management: organizing and executing around priorities and managing my emotions well."

"I like that. I'm going to write that down," Emily said. When she'd finished writing, she looked at David. "I'm guessing you have a list of your own values?"

"I do. I have five main values by which I choose to govern myself. But those are mine, and you should develop your own list."

Emily raised her eyebrows. "Sounds like an exercise in self-awareness."

"Yep." He chuckled, retrieved a piece of paper from his satchel, and handed it to Emily. On it were two columns with around twenty items in each list. "I spent some time putting this together for you. It's a values checklist of sorts, but it's not a complete list. My hope is that you'll add to it. Why don't you start with my lists and see which values resonate for you?"

Values by which I govern myself

Self-management	Gratitude
Honesty	Humility
Help-seeking	Courage
Accountability	Balance
Resiliency	Harmony
Integrity	Self-acceptance
Responsibility	Self-respect
Mindfulness	Clarity
Positivity	Faith
Flexibility	Joy
Goal achievement	Ambition

Values by which I relate to others

Compassion	Persuasive
Fairness	Teamwork
Forgiveness	Generosity
Empathy	Influence
Openness	Loyalty
Kindness	Justice
Collaborative	Love
Communicative	Care
Engaged	Motivating
Empowering	Respect
Diplomacy	Cooperation

Emily looked at the paper. He'd clearly put a lot of time into creating this document for her. She surveyed his lists, mentally checking off the values that mattered most to her.

"Wow, thank you," she said. "I can't believe you put these together. I'll define my values and add to these lists if I can." She glanced at the two values she'd written in her journal, then out at the river. "Does it ever feel like a lot of pressure? I feel like once I define these values, I really have to live them—no exceptions."

"You're not always going to live up to them," David said. "You're human. Can I tell you a story?"

Emily nodded. David told her about a time he lost $5 million, putting him and his wife $1 million in debt. He'd had financial health his whole life—never excessively wealthy but always had money in the bank. But then he made a big business bet and was defrauded. Because of the legal manipulation, he ended up losing that $5 million and going into debt.

Everyone around him said he should file for bankruptcy because it was a business failure, not a personal one, and that's really what bankruptcy laws are for. But in his heart, he knew he could pay it all back. If he filed, it would be a bankruptcy of convenience. So he plowed his way through for more than a decade and paid every penny back.

"Resiliency and accountability are values by which I choose to govern myself. If I hadn't defined those, I'm not sure I would have made the decision I made. Looking back now, I'm glad I did it that way, because character is more important than my bank account. Values guide us in times of tough decision making—through hardships. I'm not always perfect, and you won't be either." He turned to face her. "My values help me be more disciplined and accountable. They've caused me to ask for other people's help, even though it doesn't come naturally, because I've defined seeking help as a value. My values remind me of who I want to be, not just who I am."

"Wow, that's a powerful way to look at values."

"A values-first focus really shifts the way you interact with the world." He pointed to the second column on his prepared list, which Emily was holding in her left hand, a pen in her right. "Next, we have values by which you choose to relate to others. Can you think of some for you?" He saw her looking at the list, so he added, "Just off the top of your head."

Emily looked up. "Right away, I can think of one: loyalty." She created a new section in her journal and wrote down loyalty.

"What does loyalty mean to you?"

Emily studied a great blue heron as it skimmed the water, scooping up breakfast. "For me, being loyal is not looking for what I can get from people. It's sticking with them through the hard stuff."

"That's a great example. For me, loyalty means not talking about somebody when they aren't there in a way I wouldn't talk about them when they are present."

"Great definition. Give me a minute while I write that down."

David watched her finish writing. "Good. What else?"

"Well, partly because I feel like people make unfair judgments about me because of my gender, I want to be inclusive. I want to be accepting of others—not reject them because they're different." Emily wrote down *inclusive* before continuing. "And maybe another one is collaborative." She wrote that down, too.

"What does being collaborative look like?"

"I guess it means demonstrating the kindness and respect that we added to our list last time—in the character column." She wrote down *kindness* and *respect*. Emily stared at her list. "I'm not sure what else to put on there."

"Let's talk a little bit about empathy. What does it mean to you?"

"Hmm. Good question. I suppose it means you care about other people, and you're sympathetic to their situation."

"Those sound like good things, but they're not the definitions of empathy," David said.

To the point again, Emily thought. She grinned. "OK, tell me what empathy is, then."

"Empathy is the ability to see something through another person's experience, to be able to identify with the emotions they're experiencing without making any judgments about whether those emotions are right or wrong."

"That's a better definition. It actually makes me think of an example. Let's see if I can share it without getting emotional—'leading with logic,' as you would say."

The heron was back, and Emily watched it take another dive, readying herself to discuss something she didn't often share. She described a conflict she'd had with her mom a few months prior, one so deep they couldn't be in the same room for more than a few minutes without one of them getting frustrated. Her mom had criticized Emily for showing up late to a family dinner, saying Emily should find a job that doesn't require such long hours and accusing her of being overcommitted to her work. They'd gone back and forth for several minutes before her mom had stormed out of the dining room and refused to return. Since that night, Emily had talked with

Jason about the confrontation so many times she felt like her voice would give out—if her heart didn't first.

Finally, one evening after Henry had gone to bed, Jason had looked her in the eyes and said, "Em, maybe you could try listening without judging. She's angry, and you're angry. It's true you do a better job of managing your emotions, but maybe all your mom needs is to be heard."

The next day, Emily had called her mom and asked to meet. They'd sat in a quiet restaurant, and Emily listened for a full twenty minutes. She hadn't tried to justify or defend. She had simply attempted to identify with what her mom was feeling. Those twenty minutes had transformed their relationship.

Emily cleared her throat, willing away the emotion that had snuck its way into her voice as she talked. "So, yeah, I'd like to add empathy to my list. Because it changed my connection with my mom. It's definitely a value by which I want to relate to others."

"Thanks for sharing that story," David said.

Emily cleared her throat again. "Sure." Her relationship with her mom had been so fraught for months, and talking about it brought everything back up for her. Still, it showed the power of values and why they're so important to define. If she didn't define them, how would she be able to intentionally live them? She took a deep breath to clear her emotions, grateful that David was comfortable in silence.

"OK, back to our conversation," she said. "So, my homework is to define my values. I can do that . . . at least I hope so. How many?"

"No limit. I have around ten in each list, but you can have seven or twenty or however many makes sense. But here's the next home-work: Identify the five most important values in each list."

"That sounds tough. They're all so important."

"True. But here's how you might start. Pick the most important one in the list. Then, once that's chosen, pick the most important one in the list that remains, and so on until you have five. You might think about journaling about the five you choose, too. And you're probably going to change your mind a lot as you go through this activity, but at the end you've got the five that you've really given some serious thought to. And maybe in a year you'll change them again, and that's OK."

"It sounds like you're wanting me to spend a lot of time sorting through this. I trust that it's necessary, and I'll do it, but why is it so important?"

"You're right. This is hard work. But it's important because this is about who you want to become, and who you want to become as a human being is at the core of your future leadership influence, not to mention your personal relationships and parenting. Too many leaders don't define their values, and someday they get a big title and a lot of authority, but they're unsatisfied because the route they chose to get there isn't connected to how they want to govern themselves or relate to others. They haven't defined their values, and because of that, they're highly vulnerable to failure.

"Your successes are as much of a test as your failures. And you'll pass or fail those tests based on two things. First, if you know who you are, and second, if you have a clear picture of where you should be going. But if you don't know who you are, other people will define you, and they'll probably take you somewhere you shouldn't be.

"So, back to the question of 'Why is it so important?' It's important because you're going to be successful, Emily. There's no doubt in my mind. What I don't know is how you're going to handle that success, whether you'll stay rooted in your values once you make it to the top."

"I—I don't know what to say to that," Emily said. "Thank you for believing in me, and also challenging me."

"Always."

———

Emily sat on her back porch. Henry was splashing in his kiddie pool. She had to admire the kid—he could play alone for what seemed like hours. All she had to do was give him a couple dozen books inside or water of some kind outside, and he was set.

She was set, too, with her journal, a pen, and David's two lists: values by which I choose to govern myself and values by which I choose to relate to others. She'd spent some time after their meetup studying David's lists and researching values online. She'd made her initial lists, ten for governing herself and twelve for relating to others. Now, she had to determine her top five from each.

Across from her sat Jason, absorbed in emails. She knew he'd had a busy week and was still playing catch-up from all the time off he'd taken when Henry was sick. He looked up. "Everything OK? How's your nausea from earlier?"

"Oh, yeah. I'm fine. You're just so serious over there."

"Didn't you say you needed quiet to be able to think?"

Emily grinned. "Yep. I do need to focus."

"Would iced tea help?"

"You're the best."

He walked by, placing a hand briefly on her belly, and then disappeared inside. As Henry made wrecking-ball noises in his pool, Emily followed David's instructions, picking the most important value from the first list. It took her a full five minutes to decide on peace. Yes, peace was the perfect articulation of her deepest desire at home and at work—a peacefulness that extends to her motherhood and leadership. She moved on, taking her time selecting her next value: courage. When Jason emerged with iced tea, she offered a grateful smile and kept on, until she'd completed the activity five times for the values by which she chooses to govern herself.

"M-o-o-o-o-m," a voice called from twenty feet away.

"Yeah, Henry?"

"I'm a dino constructor!"

Emily laughed. "What's that, bud?"

"I'm a dino constructor! I build towers and knock them over!"

Emily watched as he stacked blocks in his pool, then put his arms out wide like a half-mummy, half-T-rex, and knocked the blocks over.

"What a silly dino constructor," Emily said. "Hey, buddy?"

"Yeah, mama?"

"Mama needs to focus for a little bit. Can you be a quiet dino constructor?"

Jason stood. "I've got it."

He retrieved the hose, attached a sprinkler, and set it up across the yard. In seconds, Henry was on to his next imaginary world.

"Thanks," Emily said as Jason settled back at his laptop.

"You bet."

She set out to complete the same activity with the other list, selecting five values by which she chooses to relate to others. The first one was easy: present. It was the thing she wanted in every interaction, with Jason and Henry, with friends and family. Her next values took more time as she considered each one carefully, eventually selecting four more. When the lists were complete, she stood. Henry was playing in the sprinklers, building "rain towers" by stacking his blocks under the water. She slid open the sliding glass door, grabbed her laptop off the kitchen counter, and returned to the patio table.

Emily opened her laptop and pulled up a text document. In it, she typed her two sets of five values. Next to each value, she included a definition.

Values by which I govern myself

- **Peace:** Speak and act in a way that brings balance and calm to my home and work; avoid unnecessary or petty disagreements. Be kind. Love people well.

- **Courage:** Do things that scare me; stand up for others who lack power or voice. Do the right thing even when it's the hard thing.

- **Curiosity:** Ask questions. Speak up when something doesn't make sense. Be a continual learner through reading, listening, and studying.

- **Determination:** When the goal is worthy, give it everything and then some.

- **Contribution:** Volunteer at least once a month and contribute financially to a cause that is meaningful to me. At home, be an equal partner in parenting and household duties.

Values by which I relate to others

- **Present:** Be mindful of the person I'm with or activity I'm doing. Be others-focused by listening, reflecting, and asking questions.

- **Loyal:** Be there for the people I care about, especially in the low points; don't talk about others behind their backs—only say things I'd say with them in the room.

- **Empathy:** Recognize my limited perspective, and treat all people like they matter. Engage Henry in conversations about what makes people different and special.

- **Collaborative:** Roll up my sleeves and jump in when needed, whether in mindshare or doing the work. In parenting, be a team member; in life, include Jason in important decisions.

- **Persuasive:** Influence others through my words and actions. Lead with logic and follow with emotion.

Then, she retyped both of the values lists David had provided and added values to each. She bolded the new items, some of which didn't make it onto her lists of five. For self: peace, curiosity, authenticity, contribution, growth, learning, adventure. For others: present, inclusive, respectful, community, equality, supportive, mentoring. Finally, she pulled up a new email.

Hi, David,

I hope you're having a nice Sunday. I spent some time working on my lists today, and I've selected my top five from each. I also added a few to your list. See attached.

You'll notice in my assignment that I went an extra step. After clarifying my values, I decided to define them. Understanding what they mean uniquely to me felt like an important part of deepening my commitment to character.

Thanks for your time yesterday. I'm really looking forward to our discussion next weekend. We'll be talking about expert leadership, right?

See you soon, and thank you, again.
Emily

She reread her message, her mouse hovering over the send button. For some reason, it was strange sending David an email, maybe because it was their first time interacting outside of their in-person meetings. Finally, she hit send and then sat quietly, watching Henry play. The kid had the best imagination—always inventing new creatures and worlds, entertaining himself in a way that felt so foreign to her at this stage in her life. He'd rekindled a creativity and love for life that she'd lost in her twenties, a time she referred to as The Pursuit because she'd been so narrowly focused on career success. Little else had mattered.

She'd had two life-openers: marrying Jason and becoming a mom. Both of her boys had opened her up, expanded her view of life, provided balance. They'd also disrupted her world, especially Henry. Caring for a baby was hard. And here she was, about to start all over again with another child.

No sleep. Endless diapers. Throw-up. Inconsolable crying. Breast pumping in the old computer room-turned-supply closet that had been halfheartedly converted into a pumping lounge. Those were the realities of having a newborn. She was going to be a zombie for at least a year, but she'd have to power through and hope Mitchell didn't decide she was unfit for her career.

Still, thanks to her meetings with David, she had a feeling of power she hadn't had before. She saw an opportunity to influence her bosses and colleagues. Glancing at the handwritten values, she realized that she'd just engaged in something important, an activity few people take the time to do. How many leaders define how they *choose* to live their lives and treat other people?

Through focusing on character leadership, she could at the very least control her behaviors by keeping them tied to her values. And if David was right, focusing on how she relates to others and governs herself would set the foundation for lasting influence that would mean more than a title or pay raise. Perhaps she could even pave the way for other women to have better experiences at work by sharing what she was learning from David.

Ding. Emily's thoughts were interrupted by an email notification. She glanced at the name: David. She hadn't expected a response so quickly! Emily clicked the email and read his reply.

Emily,

I'm impressed. You've added depth to my lists, and the values you selected show me how seriously you took this activity. I appreciate that you defined what your values mean to you, and I know you'll see the extra time investment pay off in your quest to become a character leader. Well done. I'll look forward to seeing you next weekend.

Warmly,
David

Emily caught herself smiling at her computer. She looked up, saw Jason and her dino constructor playing in the sprinkler, shut her computer, and ran over to join them.

The three played in the water for another fifteen minutes before collapsing on the grass together.

"Mommy?" Henry said.

"Yeah?"

"You're the best mommy." She met Jason's eyes before kissing Henry on top of the head.

"Thanks, bud," she said. "You're the best boy." She thought of one of her values: present. For the first time in months, she felt centered, totally aligned. She knew she'd fail—it was inevitable—but this was a good start.

No, it was a great start.

6

Who I Want to Become

"So, any insights on the values activity?" David asked. They'd been at the coffee shop for fifteen minutes and had enjoyed a surprisingly lengthy chat before David abruptly switched gears.

"I can always count on you to get us on track," Emily said.

David's face widened into a smile. "Force of habit."

"Well, you got my email. Thanks for getting back to me on a Sunday." David nodded, and Emily went on. "It was a lot of work—I think I spent at least two or three hours on it between making the longer list and narrowing them down—but it was inspiring. Not just professionally but also for who I want to become as a person. And once I'd selected my top ten values, I immediately saw an opportunity to live my values, and I acted." Emily told him about her afternoon with Henry and Jason, and how aligned she'd felt.

"It's incredible to see how you can live your values in the moment, isn't it?"

"It really is." She paused, leaning back in her chair, shoulders slightly slumped. "But I don't know how I'll ever fully become the person I defined in those lists."

"Values are aspirational. They point the way to who we want to become. It's not about perfection; it's about continual pursuit. Character isn't something you 'achieve' or 'finish.' You'll spend a lifetime building it."

"Continual pursuit. I can do that."

"Continually revisiting your values helps you avoid a breach in character. You'll continue to fall short of perfection, but it's about protecting yourself from losing all the good you've done through one moment of poor judgment."

"One moment of poor judgment?"

David nodded. "If you're not careful, you can lose all you've worked for in a moment. There are a lot of examples I could tell you of leaders who did well for years, and at some point they violated character. When that occurs, it's difficult to restore trust."

"I've seen things like that happen. My friend's boss was in the news last year for an extramarital affair with a woman in his company—it was a big scandal because they were traveling on company money and spending time together when they were supposed to be working. He'd been hugely respected before that, but after the scandal, he was fired, and I don't see how he'll ever regain respect within his industry."

"You're right. Such a major violation makes it hard to rebuild trust in people's minds and hearts."

Emily looked at the values definitions she'd brought with her. She'd printed two copies, one for her and one for David.

"I can't see myself ever doing something like that, but I do constantly fall short of these values. I was present with Henry last weekend, but yesterday morning? Not so much. I got an 'urgent'"— she put her fingers up in air quotes—"email from Mitchell at 7 a.m. And even though I chose not to respond to it because I know his fires are almost always magically dealt with an hour later with no intervention, I was distracted all morning as I got Henry ready to go."

"Like I said, character is a lifelong quest. Once you define your values, it's easier to notice when you're not living up to them. Don't beat yourself up, but do try to get better." David pointed at Emily's copy of her values. "That list is the expression of your heart. Those are the values that matter most to you in the world. One way you can stay accountable is by going through the list and ranking how you think you're living each of the values on a daily or weekly basis."

"Like a one-through-five sort of thing?"

"Exactly. One is, 'I believe in this, but I'm not living up to it.' Three is, 'I believe in it, and I'm living up to it sometimes, but I stumble.' And five is, 'I believe in it, and I'm living up to it most of the time.'"

"I'll do that this week," Emily said. "But there is one thing I do want to ask you about first. You said last time that you're going to define integrity in each of the three dimensions. We talked about values, but you never defined integrity in character leadership."

"Good catch. You're keeping me on my toes. Let me ask you, how would you define integrity in character leadership, now that you've done the hard work of defining your values?"

Emily was quiet. A full minute passed as she sorted through what she'd learned over the past weeks. "Well," she began, "based on the exercise you took me through, it would be the extent to which I'm actually living what I said my values are. Or another way to think of it is that I'm following through on the commitments I've made to myself and others."

"That's really good. Maybe you could write about that. You could even turn it into an article about making and keeping commitments."

She looked at David, surprised. "How did you know I want to start writing again?"

"Lucky guess." When Emily gave him a sideways look, he added, "It's pretty obvious you love to write. Few people put as much heart into journaling as you do."

"Well, thanks." Her cheeks reddened.

"Did I mention my oldest is a writer?" Emily shook her head.

"You didn't. Does she write professionally?"

"She does. And she's a talented writer, too." He beamed—the same expression Emily was sure she wore when Henry had learned to ride his "big boy bike." David shifted his weight, leaning forward. "One more thing I want to cover about character leaders is why people follow them."

"We talked about this earlier, didn't we? It's because they want to."

"You're right, but I want to add to it. We follow character leaders because there's something more than just a logical reason to do so. They touch a deeper part of people, at an emotional or spiritual level, and inspire loyalty." David paused. "How would you feel if people felt that way about you, Emily?"

"It's kind of scary to imagine people seeing me that way. I'm used to focusing my leadership on doing great work. But having people follow me because of my character? That seems intimidating."

"Well, this type of leadership is different. You become who you are and build your character, and people will respond to it. When you live your values, you'll naturally attract people who have similar values, and they'll follow you. And it's all the more important that you maintain your character—that you never quit striving to become the person you want to be."

Emily was quiet, wrestling within herself. She knew she wanted to live her values—to be steadfast and connected to becoming the person she wanted to become. But what David said also intimidated her. The thought of failing as a character leader seemed like a much bigger deal than anything she'd failed at in the past. If she decided to focus on character leadership in the way David was suggesting, she'd be fully dedicated to living a life of alignment. That was a big commitment.

Emily realized David was watching her, clearly waiting to hear what she had to say. "I guess if I really think about it, what's the alternative?" she said. "This is the type of leader I want to be, and if I am this leader, it sounds like I'll gain influence without seeking it."

"You're right. And it's really amazing to me that a lot of people are more afraid of success than they are of failure. They'll self-sabotage so they don't have to be in the spotlight. And I wonder: When it comes to character, how many people get close to real greatness and then back off because they're scared?"

Emily nodded. "I don't want that to be me. But I think my biggest question is, how do I keep from failing?"

"You can't. We're humans, Emily. Humans fail. The hope is that we're successful most of the time and avoid major character missteps."

"And how do I do that?"

"There are a couple of ways. One is to write your values on a little card and put it somewhere you'll see it every day. I like to keep mine on my nightstand. Every night, I ask myself, 'How well did I live these values today?' If you get in the habit of doing this so that it becomes second nature for you, it's one of the great ways you can protect yourself from ever walking away from character leadership.

"The second way is to select someone in your life who observes you often and is able to give you good feedback about how you're doing. I've asked two people to keep me accountable: my wife and a good friend. They check in with me every couple of months. We walk through each value one by one."

"Wow, really?"

"Really. It's been powerful for me as an individual but also for my marriage and friendship."

Emily shook her head, amazed. It was rare to meet someone who valued relationships so deeply. "I'm going to start with Jason. Is there a third way to stay committed?"

"The third way is to give a copy of your card to a few people who care about you—good friends who want you to succeed—and ask them to check with you regularly to ask how you're living your values. If you do those three things, you're much more likely to succeed in character leadership."

"Those are so good," Emily said. At that moment, her phone lit up. It was Jason calling. She knew he'd only call if he needed to. "Can you excuse me?"

"Of course."

Emily stood and exited into the hall behind the shop. There were big windows from the hall with a view of the tables, and as Emily answered Jason's call, she couldn't help but notice David looking straight out at the coffee shop, untethered by technology as nearly everyone else stared at screens.

Moments later, she was back at the table with David. "Sorry about that. I guess Henry is having a hard morning."

"Do you need to go?"

"No, but you know what? In the past, I would have taken that call and rushed through it. This time, I connected back to my value of presence. If I'm going to be present for you, shouldn't I also be present for Jason? And as a result, for Henry?"

"You're a quick study. Are you sure you don't need to leave?"

"I'm sure." She set her phone on the table. "Jason couldn't find Henry's favorite toy, a stuffed monkey he's had since he was a baby. I knew where it was."

"A monkey, huh? For my daughter, it was an elephant. Lady Elephant, to be exact." David's expression grew wistful.

"You have three girls and two boys, right?"

"Yes. Well, we had three boys, but my son Matthew passed at age two."

"I—I'm so sorry."

"Time heals. Or at least that's what they tell me. One of my values is resilience, and Matthew is the reason it sits in my top five and always will."

Emily reached out and put a hand on top of David's. "Thanks for sharing that with me. Do you have a picture?"

"I do," he said. He pulled out a brown leather wallet—faux leather, Emily guessed—and withdrew a small photograph of a smiling blond boy clutching a toy truck.

Emily took the picture carefully, holding it by the edges so as not to smudge the surface. She stared at the image. There was so much of Henry in this boy. "Can I ask—"

"Cancer."

"Oh." Emily handed the photo back to David. "I know it's been decades, but if there's anything I can do."

"No, this is enough for me." He gestured between them, back and forth. Emily knew what he meant. Their time together had enhanced her life, too. Not just at work, but also in her marriage and parenting. She was becoming a better person.

Emily smiled. "Coffee break?"

They walked together to the front of the shop.

As they stood in line, David said, "How about we take it to go again? I still have thirty minutes before I'm meeting my wife for brunch. We could walk for a bit."

"Great idea," Emily said.

Soon after, Emily and David had gathered their few items from the table and, with to-go cups in hand, made their way into downtown Boise.

It was ten o'clock, and Emily could see the Saturday market humming with activity a few blocks down. The two walked in silence, drinking their coffee and watching people milling past them. Finally, they reached the market.

Stopping at a jewelry booth, they leaned forward to get a better look. "My wife's birthday is coming up," David said. "But I'm not sure she'd like jewelry made of spoons." He laughed.

"I bet she would," Emily said. "My mom loves this artist."

"Really? I guess I'm out of touch with women's fashion."

Emily pointed to a wind chime made of spoons and forks. It

was rustic-looking—a country feel with a modern art twist. "How about this?"

He reached out and tapped a spoon, setting off the musical pings and dings. "She loves wind chimes. I think I'll come back after brunch so she doesn't see her present."

"Good plan."

David caught sight of a mirror just behind the earring display and gestured to it. "You know, I've never seen the back of my head."

"What?" Emily said.

"I've never seen the back of my head."

Emily stared at him and then realized what was happening. "Is there a lesson coming?"

"Might be," David said.

"Good," Emily said. She grinned. "So, the back of your head? You've never seen it."

"Well, I'm an old man, so I do the two-mirror thing every three months to see if there's a bald spot growing back there. But the reality is that I can't see the back of my head. I see a double reflection of the back of my head. And even when I look in a mirror to shave in the morning, I'm not seeing my face, I'm seeing the reflection of my face."

"I hadn't thought of it that way," Emily said. "So . . . I'll never get to see my face the way others do, from a real, human perspective. Only mirrors and photographs. And even then, I only see my face for a few minutes each day. Other people see it all day long."

"Exactly," David said. "I use the mirror as a great metaphor for character leadership, because you can never know yourself as a leader without outside help. You need people around you who can function as mirrors. And the problem is, it has to be people you trust, people who care about you, who want you to succeed, or you could end up trapped in a house of mirrors."

"I need people who keep me accountable, not ones who hold me back by offering me an inaccurate reflection of myself."

"Exactly."

The two fell into another comfortable quiet. They walked with the crowd, past the booths, eyeing the art and food. Eventually, Emily broke the silence by asking questions about David's family. He talked about his five living kids, and his wife, Dania.

"You know, I don't think I knew her name until now."

"Beautiful name, isn't it?"

"It is."

They chatted comfortably until they reached the end of the market. Finally, they stopped in front of the last booth, a stand featuring Idaho-themed art.

"I'd better get going," David said. "Brunch and my wife call."

"Are you meeting her at Big City again?"

"Of course. Best brunch spot in Boise."

"Enjoy," Emily said. "Next week, same day, same time, same place?"

"I wouldn't miss it."

They shared a quick, tight hug, and then went in different directions—David toward his car parked a few blocks over and Emily back into the market.

The crowd had thickened since they'd first started their walk. Emily let the mass drive her, staying in the little open bubble of space she occupied, walking behind a family of four with a stroller.

Family of four. That was going to be her life soon. She placed a hand on her belly, which was just starting to show if someone was looking for it.

Emily felt good. Strong. Like she was building the life she wanted for herself and her family. As though, for the first time in her career and family life, she was doing everything in her power to become who she was meant to be.

She thought back to the moment, months back, when she'd stood in the conference room after a meeting with her male colleagues. Their dirty coffee cups, their askew chairs. How could she have known, in that moment, that the war she'd waged wasn't so much against them but instead within herself?

She'd come so far in such a short period of time. The anger had abated, and in its place was hope. Because instead of seeking a promotion, she now sought to live her values. She desired influence, not power. She knew—she just *knew*—that if she stayed true to the desires of her heart, and stopped focusing on a promotion, she'd rise in the company.

But still, she needed to have a tough conversation with Mitchell. He needed to understand that his biases were not OK. But when? And how?

Emily arrived at her bike, undid the chain, and put on her helmet. Her two guys were waiting for her, and she couldn't wait to tell them about her morning.

7

Next, Become an Expert

Emily made her way into the coffee shop ten minutes early and headed upstairs to claim a table before ordering. Given David's track record, she expected a few minutes to herself before he got there, but she was wrong.

"David!" Emily said.

He laughed. "You sound surprised to see me."

"I am—I mean, I'm not. You're usually a bit . . . late."

"I'm typically quite punctual. I've been off lately, but I'm back. How are you doing today?"

"I won't be better until this thing is out of me," she said with a laugh. "Kidding. But really, I am starting to see the other side of nausea."

"I'm happy to hear that."

"And I'm starting to show." She placed her hand on her belly. "It's about time to tell Mitchell and my team."

"Are you feeling good about that conversation?"

"You know, a few weeks ago, I would have said no way. But now I feel—how do I explain it? I guess I feel confident about myself, my values, my ability to influence. And all of that makes me confident about this baby. That I can have the life I want at home and at work." Emily paused. "Jason's feeling more confident too."

"Oh, yeah?"

"Yeah. All of the coaching you've been giving me, well, I've been sharing the highlights with him. I think he was more nervous than me about this baby, partially because he sometimes takes on more of the parenting load. But my confidence has increased his confidence. It's been a growing experience for both of us."

Emily shared how, after their last meeting, she'd sat on the back patio with Jason. Henry had been having a tough few weeks, so it was the first time they'd been able to sit down and have a real conversation in days. After she had detailed the first dimension of leadership, character, Jason had looked at her and said, "I noticed there was a difference in you, and I wondered where it was coming from."

"It was the best compliment," Emily said to David. "He asked to see my values, and said he'd make his own lists. We talked about our work, and what this baby means for our lives. It was the most meaningful talk we've had in months."

David's face wrapped in a broad smile. "I am so glad."

"Me too. Now, enough sappy stuff. Let me go order my coffee and let's get to it."

Minutes later, Emily was back upstairs. She sat across from David at one of the long tables.

"Expert leadership," she said.

"That's right."

Emily nodded toward him. "Take it away."

He let out a short laugh. "All right. Well, you can have great character, but no company will hire you if you don't have skills or knowledge," he said. "You have to actually be able to accomplish something. Expert leadership is the influence you have because of what you can do or what you know. People will give you power—they'll freely follow you as an expert leader if you know how to do something they need or if you can solve problems they have."

"Like my obstetrician. Or my mechanic."

"Exactly." David went on to share how he'd recently gone to the dermatologist for a routine visit when his doctor noticed something on the edge of his nose. The doctor had gone across the room to grab something, and the next thing David knew, she was coming at him with a blowtorch. The blowtorch ended up being liquid nitrogen, 321 degrees below zero, and David had to decide, do I trust this person? For about a week, he wasn't sure he'd made the right decision because his nose had a large wound that wasn't healing well.

"As a matter of fact, it looked a lot worse than before she messed with it. But it's all cleared up now, so today, I'm glad I trusted her."

"Because she's an expert in skin," Emily said. "But you wouldn't have trusted her to work on your teeth."

"Right. And I've also learned that she's not an expert in healing naturally. After a few experiences of being prescribed medication I either didn't need, or I didn't need as much of, I've learned to trust her in some things and not other things. Or to at least do my homework before I blindly follow her lead."

"You know, that's been my experience with a lot of medical

providers. But our pediatrician regularly exceeds my expectations as an expert leader. Once, I brought in a scientific study, and not only did she take the time to read it, but she called me later that week to follow up. She even works with a naturopathic doctor to find more natural approaches to treating her patients."

"It sounds like she shows you respect and is willing to consider that maybe she doesn't know it all."

"When I think about it, she's a great combination of both an expert and a character leader."

"You know, we talk about the two as separate things, but you can't really separate them. They work together. Any other expert leader examples you can think of?"

"My accountant. I follow him because I trust him, and I know his ethics well enough that if he recommends something, I don't question it. I know he's going to protect me. Same with my attorney."

"Exactly," David said. "It's similar in the workplace. The person who's in charge of marketing or designing a new microchip or managing a cross-functional team—those are all examples of expertise. They may have a position or title attached to them, but we're not following the position. We're letting the person influence because of what they know or what they can do. So, that's the second dimension, expert leadership."

"That's great, David. But you said we're going to define integrity here, too."

"Straight to the point."

Emily smiled. "I learned from the best."

"The first way to define integrity in expert leadership is, does my expertise actually create real value for others? Does it improve someone's life, solve a problem, or help them advance in some way?

Because it's not really leadership expertise if it's not creating something for others."

"Makes sense."

"The second way to define integrity in expert leadership is, are you staying fresh and relevant? Are you continuing to grow? Maintaining integrity in expertise means staying current. The world is changing too fast to depend on yesterday's knowledge."

"That's so true. I just read an article the other day that said human knowledge is doubling every twelve months! And in my business, if I don't keep learning, I'll become obsolete really fast."

"I think I read that article while I was having coffee here the other day. Did you see the other prediction that human knowledge will eventually double every twelve hours? It could even happen in your lifetime."

Emily shook her head in disbelief. "So that's two: creating value and staying current. Is there a third way to define integrity in expert leadership?"

"Yes. The third is, are you looking for ways you can create new expertise to make you more valuable to your team, company, boss, client—whoever?"

"What do you mean?"

"Well, do you know anyone on your team who is studying the trends in society that could potentially have a direct impact on the future success or failure of your business?"

Emily thought for a moment. "No one comes to mind. What trends do you mean?"

"There are trends so big they can affect all of us one way or another. One of those trends is demographics, like generational shifts—younger leaders coming into the workplace. Other trends are health care or globalization. Any of those will have a big impact on your industry and company. One of the ways you can develop new expertise beyond the expertise you have today is by identifying a trend that will impact your company in the future, five or ten years from now. Then, you can begin to develop your own expertise in those areas. And if you do, and if you speak up in a few opportune moments and mention that you've been reading about that trend, do you think that would give you more influence?"

"I think it would," Emily replied, then grinned. "And then they might even listen to a woman."

David laughed. "Maybe so."

"OK, so I need to define areas I'm already an expert in, and figure out ways to develop those areas even more. I also need to study a trend that will impact my company. Now I just need to figure out how to do all that."

"I have an idea you could mull over. It's really the same way people get PhDs. When you get a PhD, there are essentially three main segments."

David went over the stages of a PhD. First, it involves studying other thought leaders—reading or listening to people who have been recognized as advancing that body of knowledge. The second stage is to write a dissertation, and the question is, how are you going to add to the body of knowledge that exists in your field of expertise? A PhD candidate has to come up with a thesis, an experiment, and some research—an idea that will create new insights, knowledge, or innovation in their field of expertise.

The third stage of a PhD is to submit it to other people who are peers and experts to critique the dissertation. These individuals get to decide if the dissertation is scientifically valid and adds real insight to the field. Every PhD process is a combination of those three things.

"What if, as part of your ongoing integrity in expertise, you decide to earn a self-study PhD every three to five years?" David asked. "You could pick one targeted area of expertise where you want expert influence and go deeper than anybody else in the company. You'd create your own strategic learning plan, study all the thought leaders, and think about what they have to say.

"And over time, you'll develop some novel concept or new idea in that area of expertise. You'll test it, experiment with it, then ask people you respect who are experts to challenge it and critique whether or not you've come up with something new."

Emily's mind was already going in ten directions, trying to figure out what she might choose to focus on. Suddenly, she knew. "Advancing women in technology."

David straightened in his chair. "Tell me more."

"I'd love to learn about the challenges women face, the advantages they have, and how the industry can support women in leadership."

"That's great, Emily. Just great. So, how could you become the smartest person in the room on that specific topic?"

Emily suggested creating a list of thought leaders on the topic of women in technology, then reading or listening to what they have to say, or even attending conferences they're speaking at. "Or maybe I could even reach out to one of them and ask if they'd be willing to mentor me because I want to be an expert in this area as well," she said. "And I was just thinking, too, that the women's leadership group I'm a part of will be a great forum for exploring what I've learned and challenging what I'm adding to the dialogue."

"Excellent ideas. Why don't you work on building that into a clear set of action steps you're going to take. And be sure to ask three questions. First, who is this going to benefit? Because remember, integrity in expertise begins by creating value for someone else."

"OK, got it. Good reminder. It's not just for myself—it's for my company and other women."

"Second, you need to ask, how can I stay current? You've answered this already by your plan to study and reach out to relevant thought leaders. And the third question is, what new expertise could I create in the future?"

"I'm not sure I have the answer to that yet."

"That's OK. You can't know what to add until you know what's out there. I'm confident it will come to you as you work on this."

"I'm open to the fuzziness of this activity," Emily said. She shook her head. "I never thought I'd be open to fuzziness. I usually like to know where I'm going and how I'll get there. This is new for me."

"Openness is a good thing. It means you're growing."

"That I am."

Emily looked at her watch. "Oh! It's 10:45. No market today?"

"Dania had some errands, so we're meeting at eleven."

"Does that mean we have time to talk about the third dimension?" Emily leaned forward. She wanted to squeeze every drop of information out of him she could. These meetings were wonderful, but she wished they could be daily. She couldn't learn fast enough.

"Not today. I want you to get a clear picture of where you're going with expert influence. Depending on how your learning plan comes together, maybe next time we'll talk about positional leadership."

Emily sat back in her chair, not hiding her disappointment. "I'll be done by next week, I promise you that. I'm eager to learn about the last dimension."

"I'd better get going." David stood, and Emily jumped up to walk him to the door, leaving her journal and purse behind to save her spot.

She noticed he was moving a little slowly, but the bags had disappeared from under his eyes and he seemed to be doing well. She had to remind herself that he was in his seventies—sitting with him these mornings, she felt like she was talking to a sharp and focused forty-year-old. His body might be slowing down but his mental capacity sure wasn't.

"David," Emily said once they were out the door and standing in the warm early summer morning air, "I was wondering"—she hesitated, looking down the street at the people making their way to the market, then back at David—"would you and Dania want to come to Henry's birthday party next week? I'd really love for you to meet my family."

"I'd be honored," David said without hesitation. "When is it?"

"Tuesday after next at four o'clock."

"We'll be there."

Emily's mouth upturned into smile. "I can't wait." She reached out and grabbed his hand. "Thanks again, David. These mornings mean so much to me."

"Me too." He gave her hand a light squeeze before turning to leave.

Emily watched David's figure retreat into downtown Boise before she turned back toward the coffee shop. Suddenly, her stomach lurched, and she felt bile rise into her throat. She broke into a half-run, half-sprint through the shop and into the bathroom.

As she wiped her face and washed her hands a few minutes later, she looked at herself in the mirror. Her face was colorless, but her eyes were bright. At least there was a good reason for her sickness.

She made her way back to her now-solo table, sat down in David's chair, and took out her journal. Half an hour later, Emily looked up from her writing. Her strategic learning plan was done. Becoming an expert on women in technology was a big commitment, but she knew it would be worth the effort.

Her neck felt tight. She stretched her head back as far as it would go, bent her chin toward her chest, and then moved her head from side to side. Writing by hand wasn't something she was used to, and it had been an adjustment sitting in a position that didn't require two hands on a computer keyboard. Looking at her journal, she surveyed what she'd written.

Strategic Learning Plan

1. *Identify thought leaders on the topic of women in technology, especially women leaders in technology. Create a research document that lists their name, area of influence/research, a short description of their contribution to the field (research, activism, etc.), and a list of their publications (books, articles, talks, etc.).*

2. *Narrow the list to ten people I want to study closely. Spend one to two weeks studying each thought leader in depth.*

3. *Reach out to the most compelling thought leader to request mentorship. If she declines, ask another. Travel to meet with mentor or attend an event she's speaking at.*

4. *Identify how I'll contribute to the field (deliver talk, write article . . . book?).*

Three Questions

1. *Who is this going to benefit? Building my expertise will directly benefit my company and especially the women within the company by bringing current learning to the organization. As I become an expert, I may get to influence policy within the company to better support women. My hope is to someday impact other women in tech outside of my company too.*

2. *How can I stay current? In addition to studying thought leaders, I'll continue seeking out current news related to women in tech.*

3. *What new expertise could I create in the future? I don't know, but I'm open.*

She used a scanning app on her phone to capture her handwritten plan and then emailed it to David with the subject, "Emily's self-directed PhD strategic learning plan."

Emily glanced at her watch. She had fifteen more minutes of peace and quiet before Jason and Henry would be meeting her downtown, and she was going to make the most of it. She put her phone away, switched her watch to do not disturb, and looked out at the shop in thought.

No distractions. No technology. Just her and her mind—an exercise in being like David, the greatest leader she'd ever met.

8

Let's Talk about Structural Leadership

E mily sat across the conference table from Mitchell, waiting for him to finish an email he was writing on his laptop. They'd agreed to meet in the conference room to save Mitchell transition time since he had another meeting there in thirty minutes. In the still silence, the sound of his keys reverberated throughout the room, and Emily felt an urge to reach into her bag, withdraw her earplugs, and block out the noise.

Mitchell hit the delete button at least a dozen times, looked up, and said, "It'll just be a moment."

"Take your time," Emily replied.

She looked out the conference room window at the sweeping view of her beloved city. Boise was especially beautiful this morning, the mountains crisp blue and white and the foothills a warm green. The hills would be a perfect place to run this weekend, with the wildflowers and green grasses, though she knew her allergies wouldn't agree. And her nausea probably wouldn't, either.

Of course, she had to remember not to mention the pregnancy to Mitchell—that announcement would come soon, but she wasn't ready quite yet.

She glanced over at Mitchell, who was still engrossed in his email, and then stood, walked over to the window, and stared down at the street below. People didn't seem to be in a hurry this morning. She saw a couple walking their dog, coffees in their hands. A few paces behind them was a runner, who passed widely to the left of the couple. A dad and his toddler were walking hand in hand, and she saw the man stop, kneel down to talk to his daughter, and then stand and scoop her up to sit on his shoulders. Emily smiled at the two, thinking of Jason and Henry, and wondering if their new addition might be a daughter.

"OK, I'm . . . almost . . . done," Mitchell said. Emily made her way to her seat as he closed his laptop. "Sorry about that."

"No problem. Putting out another fire?"

"Not a fire—just something to do with the potential acquisition."

"I see."

"So, why did you want to talk today?"

Emily breathed in and out imperceptibly, pulling in the courage she needed and exhaling fear. "I have some questions I want to ask. First, I'm wondering if you can tell me what you think my strengths are at Enertec—as a leader and team member."

Mitchell looked at her for a moment, as though he was trying to decide if that was really the question or if there was something buried underneath her inquiry. Finally, he said, "You know, you do an excellent job around here. One of the things I value about you is that I can rely on you to get things done. You have energy and enthusiasm that maybe even surpasses my own, if I'm being honest." He paused in thought before continuing. "And you're smart. Everyone knows that. You think a lot, and I've noticed you're growing yourself as a leader and person."

Emily's eyes widened at his compliments, but she kept her composure. "Wow, Mitchell. I don't know what to say. Thank you."

Mitchell nodded. Emily went on, "Now, my next question: What can I do to improve?"

It took Mitchell longer to answer this question. He grabbed his pen and held it with both hands, as if it contained an answer. Finally, he looked up. "I think the biggest thing is to grow others. I know I can rely on you, but I don't always feel like I can rely on your team. I notice you picking up their slack sometimes, and I'd like to see you inspire and train the people below you to perform at the same level as you."

Emily was nodding as she considered what he said. She knew it was important to listen to Mitchell if she wanted him to listen to her. "I had no idea you thought that. But, you know, you're right. When I think about it, sometimes I do pick up the slack when I'd be better off handing things back to the people on my team and helping them learn how to do the job right. I get worried about the ball getting dropped, but maybe the ball can be strategically dropped."

Mitchell leaned forward. He placed his elbows on the table and set his chin on his thumbs, his fingers interlaced in front. "Why do you ask?"

Emily looked him straight in the eyes. "I've been trying to understand our last conversation. Why I'm not getting promoted and my male colleagues are."

He straightened his spine, palms flat on the table in front of him. "I've been thinking about our conversation too."

"Do you understand my confusion? I think I outperform them nine out of ten times."

"You're talented. There's no doubt there. But I told you, my concern—leadership's concern—is that you're torn between two worlds, and the demands of a promotion might not be the best decision. We'd rather you excel where you are than promote you and see you fail."

"What in my history makes you think I'll fail?"

Mitchell drew his forehead inward in thought. "I guess nothing."

"Do you have the same concerns about male leaders with children?"

He looked at her in surprise. "No. No, I don't."

"Don't you think I should be the one to decide whether or not to take on more demands at work and whether I can handle it all?"

Mitchell studied her momentarily, then turned in his chair and looked out the window.

"Mitchell?"

He turned to face her. "I heard you."

Emily held her posture and steadied her jaw. "Well?"

"I get what you're saying. You think I'm discriminating because you're a woman."

"No, I don't think that." Emily met his eyes. "I know that."

Mitchell's face tightened, his brows drawing in toward his nose, his jaw set. Emily kept his gaze, refusing to back down. A full minute passed, the quiet crowded with thoughts. Suddenly, his expression softened and his jaw relaxed.

"From the outside looking in, I can see how your not getting a promotion could seem . . . discriminatory." He grabbed at the collar of his shirt. She almost felt sorry for him. "Please know I never had any intention of doing that to you."

"But you did, Mitchell. You did. And here I am, years behind other men because you and other leaders decided motherhood was a liability. There should not be different standards for me because I'm a woman."

His head dropped. She wondered if he was more concerned about her or what might happen to him if she reported the discrimination. Awkwardness ballooned between them as Mitchell shifted in his seat once, then twice. Finally, he said, "What do you want to do?"

"Look, Mitchell. I'm not here to get you in trouble. I'm here to influence your thinking. I want things to change around here, not just for me but for other women. I want you to be an advocate." She stopped talking, waiting for Mitchell to meet her gaze before continuing. "But know that if things don't change, I won't hesitate to report you—and the men above you."

A silence fell over them as Mitchell turned again to look out the window. Finally, he spoke. "How are you so calm about this? Now that I see this from your perspective, I can't believe you're not yelling at me."

"I've been learning to lead with logic and follow with emotion," she said. "And if I'm being honest, I was mad. I'm still mad. I just chose to wait until the time was right to talk with you."

"Lead with logic and follow with emotion," Mitchell echoed. "I like that."

"I learned it from a wise friend."

The two stood, and Emily made her way to the door. Before she exited the room to return to her office, Mitchell spoke once more. "Emily?"

"Yeah?"

"I have a lot to think about."

Emily opened her mouth to speak but no words came out. The two stared at each other in silence. Finally, she nodded. Mitchell offered a low wave goodbye and took his seat again to wait for his next meeting.

Emily walked back to her office, closed the door, and stood on the other side, her back against the cool wood. Would confronting Mitchell make a difference? She couldn't see the future, but at least she was finally influencing it.

⌒

Emily looked around her house, mentally checking off the to-do items for Henry's party. The time on the microwave read 3:42. Food was set out on their kitchen island: her much-requested slow-cooker spinach and artichoke dip, fresh berries and watermelon from the farmer's market, an assortment of cheeses and crackers, and her favorite, Jason's brownies. A wading pool had been blown up and filled, and Jason was out on the patio with Henry, loading a cooler with cold drinks. Decorations had been hung, presents wrapped. All she could do now was wait.

Why was she so nervous? All of their usual guests would be there, but two were new: David and Dania. Two Ds—she'd never noticed the alliteration of their names. Somehow, it fit what she knew about them, the connectedness and compatibility they seemed to share. Their marriage, or at least her perception of it, was something she aspired to emulate.

The back door slid open, pulling her from her thoughts, and Jason and Henry walked inside. She bent over and kissed Henry on the head. "Are you excited for your party?"

"Yeah! Can I have a brownie?"

Jason laughed as Emily shook her head. "Let's wait for our guests."

"Can I go wait at the window?" Henry said, wiggling with excitement.

"Sure, birthday boy. Let me know if you see anyone."

Emily and Jason watched their boy run to the front of the house and stand in the tall bay windows overlooking the front yard.

"You OK?" Jason asked. He leaned on the kitchen counter, his right hip against the edge. "I saw you standing in the kitchen just staring. You've been holding that bag of chips for about five minutes."

"Huh?" Emily looked down, surprised, then opened the bag and poured it into an empty bowl on the island. "Oh, yeah. Yep. I'm good."

Jason took the empty bag from Emily, tossing it into the garbage can they'd set out for guests to use. "You're nervous about David coming over, aren't you?"

"A little." She met his eyes. "More excited, I think."

"I get the excitement, but why are you nervous? Haven't you spent a lot of time with him already?"

"We've only gone to coffee and taken walks. Everything has been centered around work. A little chit-chat here and there. But coming to my house? Meeting you? Me meeting his wife? I don't know. It's just different."

"I know you respect him a lot. Just remember, he's coming because he respects you, too. Just be you."

"I know. You're right." She shook her body quickly, dramatically, and laughed. "I'm shaking it off."

Jason smiled and gave her a tight squeeze on her upper arm. "It'll be great."

Just then, the doorbell rang. Emily's mom and dad stood at the door, each loaded with gifts. Their arrival seemed to open the floodgates for other guests, because the home was soon filled with about thirty people. Finally, around 4:15, the last guests arrived.

"David!" Emily said as she opened the door. "And you must be Dania. This is Jason, my husband, and our son, Henry." Emily reached out her hand, but Dania swept her into a warm embrace, then did the same with both Jason and Henry.

David shook Jason's hand then knelt down to Henry's eye level. "And this must be the birthday boy."

As Emily watched the group say hello, she admired Dania's silver hair tied back in a tight bun, long, eclectic earrings, and silk parachute pants. She remembered the bag David carried, and it all clicked. This lady had style.

"David's told me so much about you and your family," Dania said. "I feel like I know you already."

"I feel the same about the two of you," Jason said.

"Me too!" Henry yelled, jumping in the air and pumping his fist.

"Oh! I almost forgot," David said. He reached into Dania's handbag and pulled out a package. "This is for you, Henry."

"A present!" Henry jumped up and down as David handed him the gift.

"You can go put that in your present pile, bud," Jason said. He looked at David and Dania. "Thank you both. That was nice of you."

Emily guided the group through the house and introduced the newly arrived guests to their friends and family. As she watched David and Dania, she noticed a special kind of energy between them, something she had only witnessed a handful of times in her life. Was it respect? Contentment? Yes, but there was something else.

Dania laughed and clutched David's arm, and Emily realized what they shared: ease and kindness. It was clear they not only loved each other but preferred each other—not just above others, but above themselves. Admiration. She felt that way about Jason, but she wasn't sure she expressed it so openly.

Soon, it was time for brownies and presents. The group gathered to sing to Henry and watch him tear into his gifts with unmatched ferocity.

An hour later, the birthday crowd had thinned. Dania was deep in conversation with Emily's parents, and Jason and a few close friends were sitting on the back patio, relaxing while the kids played in the kiddie pool. Emily stood in the kitchen, watching through the window as Henry splashed in the water.

David made his way over to Emily. She turned toward him as he approached, gesturing out at the backyard.

"Isn't childhood magical?"

David nodded. "It sure is. This has been fun. Thank you for inviting us."

"I'm really glad you came."

"So am I."

The two were quiet, watching the kids run through the sprinkler, then back into the pool. Finally, David spoke.

"I know we're not on 'official business' today," he said, "but I can't help asking: Did you talk with your boss?"

Emily had been holding in the news of her discussion with Mitchell for more than a week, starting and trashing nearly a half-dozen emails to David. She knew it would be much more fun to tell him in person about the exchange with her boss. The party was basically over, and everyone else was occupied, so it seemed like the perfect time to share.

"I did. I'd love to tell you about it. Shall we sit?"

David agreed, and they walked across the long backyard to a bench swing nestled under a large willow.

Less than a minute after they'd sat down, Emily launched into her story. She recalled the conversation with Mitchell and his unexpected reaction. Her cheeks flushed with pride and excitement as she finished her story. Even though it had been a difficult discussion, she knew she'd handled it well. She'd had the conversation at the right time. She'd led with logic and followed with emotion.

"And yesterday, I went in to tell him about this little one," she went on, patting her expanding belly. "When I was pregnant with Henry, that had been an awkward conversation. This time, it wasn't. I could tell Mitchell made a conscious effort not to react to my announcement. He even congratulated me and said he'd work hard to make sure the team supported my maternity leave."

"Wow. That's a big statement coming from him."

"I know. I feel like I've said what I needed to say. I've proven myself. I've called his bias out, and he acknowledged it. Honestly, this baby couldn't come at a better time."

"How so?" David asked. He'd been listening quietly throughout Emily's story, giving her the space to celebrate.

"Well, when I first found out about the baby, I thought it would be a career setback. Don't get me wrong—I was excited. I just know what babies have done to other women's careers; or, I guess, what male leaders have done to other women's careers because they had babies. It was hard enough with Henry, but two kids? It was . . . I was overwhelmed. Now, I feel like I'm allowed to just be excited. No more guessing, no more pretending things are OK at work when they're not. In some ways, it will be a good challenge, a test to see how Mitchell and the company respond. I'm doing everything I can to grow. Now, it's their turn."

David looked at Emily as though he was searching for just the right thing to say. Their eyes met for a stretched moment, Emily offering a warm smile and David reciprocating. Suddenly, her throat caught as she noticed the deep pride in David's expression. This whole process had been a struggle for her, but now she realized how much he'd felt it with her. The discussion with Mitchell was a triumph. She was finding her way with David as her guide.

Their friendship was familiar, a mix of friend and father, brother and confidant—combinations that were hard to explain but easy to feel.

The two turned simultaneously and looked out across the yard, the kids now huddled masses on the porch, wrapped in towels and eating watermelon. Emily's throat was still tight, holding in the emotional weight she'd been carrying for the past several months.

She heard David clear his throat. "Emily," he finally said, turning once again to meet her eyes. "I am so proud of you."

Emily's eyes welled. She fanned her face. "Darn pregnancy hormones." David's eyes reddened, and he blinked quickly, rubbing his right eye with his index finger.

"I don't have that excuse," he said.

Emily laughed. "OK, enough of this emotional stuff. Shall we head back to the party?"

"Yep. Let's go see that boy of yours."

—

The following Saturday, Emily had just parked her bike outside Slow by Slow when she saw David approaching in the distance. She waved, walking to meet him.

"Good morning!" she called.

David waved back. "Morning!"

As the two walked into the coffee shop, they talked about Henry's party, Emily sharing how much Henry had loved the books David and Dania had brought him. They ordered, opting to wait for their coffee rather than have it brought up.

As they sat down at a two-person table, Emily looked at David. "OK, it's been too long since my last leadership lesson."

David chuckled. "Good point."

"Last time, we covered expert leadership, and I sent you my strategic learning plan."

"Yes, and I want to talk about your plan. But before that, any other updates?"

"Just a couple. First, our virtuous conspiracy is still going strong. Karen was our initial honoree, and I think we've narrowed down the next two. We've been focusing on lifting up people who are newer in their careers or leadership, and there's someone on my team I hope we get to honor soon. Our group hasn't quite gotten into a regular rhythm yet, but I know we'll get there."

"Great. And your discretionary time?"

"I'm struggling a bit, but I'm making progress. I'd say I'm averaging three days a week right now."

"What's been keeping you from five days?"

"I'm just so tired," Emily said, her hand on her stomach. "I feel like I need to prioritize self-care right now. I'm trying to find a good balance."

David tilted his head to one side in thought. "You know, that's amazing."

"What's amazing?"

"It's so easy to see the world through my own context and experience. And because I've never been pregnant, I'm totally oblivious to what that experience is like. Thanks for helping me see another aspect of what it means to work within the circle of control." Emily dipped her head in a mock bow, which made David chuckle. "OK, now how about your PhD?"

"I have a list going right now—an annotated bibliography of sorts. I have thirteen on my list, and I'm working to identify at least that many more."

"Good work. Your plan was exceptional, by the way."

"Really? Even though it's incomplete? I'm still stumped about what I can add to the field."

"That'll come. It's nearly impossible to know what that is from the outset."

"OK, last update. Ready for this?" Emily's eyes narrowed and she lifted one eyebrow, as if holding a great secret. David nodded. "Mitchell promoted Tara, a woman on my team. She's a level below me and has deserved a promotion for months. I think I'm more excited about her promotion than if it had been my own."

"Wonderful."

"It really is. The best part is that she has three kids, and the youngest is still an infant. I'm pretty sure that has never happened in the history of the company."

David shook his head in admiration. "Incredible. And with that news, I think it's time we talk about integrity in the third dimension of leadership, positional leadership."

Emily rubbed her hands together in excitement. "Finally! OK, so we've covered two of the three dimensions: character leadership and expert leadership. Now, we're discussing positional leadership. Did you call it structural leadership before?"

"I did. Positional, or structural, leadership."

"I'm ready. I've been waiting months to learn this."

David assumed his executive demeanor: posture straight, forearms resting on the table, hands clasped. His gaze was sharp as he spoke. "The first thing to understand is that people follow the position, not the person, when it comes to structural leadership. They follow because of the power or authority of the position within the organization. The bigger the position, the more they'll follow the position instead of the person. And that position has to be given to the person in it; positional leadership is always based on external endorsement."

"OK, so a CEO has to be hired. But what if the CEO founded the company? No one gives them that role—no one endorses them."

"Even entrepreneurs need to be legitimized by the state. They're granted their position by the state they live in."

"Ah, good point. Would another example of a positional leader be the president of the United States?"

"Exactly."

"OK, makes sense. A positional leader requires outside endorsement, and people follow the position, not the person. Is there ever a time that a person becomes bigger—or, I guess, more important—than the position?"

"What a positional leader says, their demeanor, and how they present themselves—all of this is amplified either for better or for worse. So, if you use the right words, and have a positive demeanor and presence, you're bigger than life, in a good way. And if you use the wrong words, and have a negative demeanor and presence, you're bigger than life . . . and that's to the detriment of the people who follow you."

Emily was quiet, taking in David's words as he continued. He explained that positional leadership is temporary; it doesn't last forever. Everyone will eventually lose that dimension of leadership, and sometimes it's because of poor performance, because they've disappointed others. Other times, it's because it's time to move on. Either they get another opportunity, they retire, or there's some other mitigating factor, but everybody leaves.

"Can I tell you one of my stories?" David asked.

"Please," Emily replied.

David shared that when he was a CEO, he traveled the world.

While doing site inspections for conventions, he'd be picked up by limos and brought to big suites with chocolates and flowers waiting for him. He'd have great meals rolled out by people who were trying to gain his influence, and it was always "mister" this and "sir" that. While it was amazing treatment, David knew it wasn't for him. It was for the position. And he wasn't the position, he was just occupying it.

"And then, after I retired, I said to our leadership team, 'In six months, you guys won't remember who I am. And I guarantee you I'll no longer be competent for this business, because things change so fast I'll have lost touch with what's going on.' And it took about six months for people to realize I was not that leader anymore, and they began to relate to me differently."

"Surely they didn't forget you."

"No. But they forgot me as the CEO. They eventually saw me as Dave, their friend, rather than David, their leader."

David went on, telling of a time he vacationed with his wife at one of the hotels he had visited multiple times while he was the CEO. When he arrived, not only did no one recognize him, but there were numerous issues with his room, and his wife was refused service at the spa for lack of an appointment—even though she'd made an appointment three months earlier and had the email to prove it. There was no apology, and while the room issues were fixed, no grand gestures were made to restore their experience. Even though it was a disappointing experience, David laughed out loud when the bellhop watched them carry their bags to their rental car parked out front.

"What was so funny?" Emily asked.

"A year prior, I had a dedicated staff person who sent me a gift basket every day. I received handwritten notes from the hotel manager and chef-special dinners at their finest restaurant. I couldn't help but laugh at the difference. There I was, loaded up with my wife's and my suitcases, with a satchel on my shoulder, struggling under the weight of the bags. The difference was so striking, I began to laugh." At this, David's face broke out in a broad smile. "My wife looked at me like I was crazy, and then she started laughing too. I'm pretty sure any thoughts the bellhop had of helping us quickly disappeared.

"So, I was chuckling on the way out. The year before, I was the CEO of an international company where I got treated like royalty everywhere I went. Now, I was being ignored. And I think it's just a great example of how none of us hold a position forever."

Emily was grinning, imagining the scene and wondering what the bellhop had been thinking. "That really puts it into perspective, doesn't it?"

"It does," David said. "But don't misunderstand me. When you get promoted, and you will, you should feel great. It's just important to remember that the position is bigger than you. Don't delude yourself into thinking you are the position. You've been given the opportunity to serve in the position."

"Hmm. I'd never thought of it that way," Emily said. She tilted her head back slightly and looked up at the ceiling in thought. "OK, so, eventually everybody leaves. Some leave because of poor performance; others, because it's time to move on. I don't ever want to leave because of poor performance, so how does integrity come into play?"

"Good question. Three things are important for you to understand

and continually reflect on about the position you're given in the company. The first is, what are the rules of the position?"

"What do you mean, 'rules'?"

"A lot of times, the position indicates where you can go find the rules. So, you want to become a director. The first place you'd look for the rules for becoming a director would be to ask if there's a position description for the director role, because it should have some of the rules for that position. Another place to look is the employee handbook, because there are certain rules everybody who's an employee of the company has to live by. The handbook will have rules about benefits, vacation time, things like that. But it could also have rules about legitimate expenses to turn in for reimbursement."

Emily nodded. "That makes me think of a CFO at one of our competitors who was fired by his board of directors. It wasn't because he wasn't doing a good job—actually, the company was having a record year. But he was turning in expense receipts for things that he shouldn't, like personal trips and expensive meals that weren't work-related. When the board found out, they fired him."

"Sounds like he ignored the rules of the handbook—rules I'm certain he knew—and the unwritten rules of morality. Integrity involves not just knowing the rules but choosing to follow them."

"Exactly. It was such an avoidable situation." Emily leaned back in her chair. "So, employee handbook and position description. Is there anywhere else I should go for the rules?"

"Depending on the business or organization, sometimes there may be governmental rules you have to follow, so the Department of Labor is one place to look. If you're a director traveling overseas, it's important to understand the US government's rules on interacting with foreigners. If you're a board member, oftentimes the bylaws of the organization define what rules you need to live by. When you get this next promotion, it's important to start by finding out what the rules of the job are, and then follow those rules."

Emily pulled her notebook from her bag and began writing. She looked up. "Got it. Notes made. What else?"

David shook his head, amused at her eagerness. "OK, moving on. The second way we can define integrity for positional leadership is measuring expected key results. Those results might have to do with financial numbers, or they might be connected to certain practices and policies. Just like you identified your values, it's also helpful to list the key results of the position you're occupying. Most positions have three to five key results. If you achieve those key measures, it's unlikely that you'll be removed for not getting results in that job. And there's a process you can go through to define what those results are for your specific position."

"This is helpful. Can you share the process?"

David explained that the first thing is to ask people who work closely with the position what they think those results might be. For a director, that might mean talking with a VP or even the CEO, depending on the reporting structure in the organization. It might be other directors who can help clarify what results are expected.

"And it's also important to ask the question, 'What results do my subordinates expect from me?' Because really, it's the people all around you, a 360-degree view of the role and understanding what people expect from you, that define integrity in the position."

"Three to five results . . . that doesn't seem like enough. With all that feedback, wouldn't I end up with a lot more?"

"You're right. You'll end up with a longer list. And yet all of my experience has taught me that if you aim for more than three to five big results in your job, you're probably going to fail. It's similar to your values. If you make a list of twenty values and never narrow it down, it will be hard to stay focused on the most important ones. Likewise, if you aim for more than five key results for a position, it's easy to become overwhelmed and distracted by the enormous list of expectations."

"Makes sense."

"My advice is to spend time identifying three to five key results of the director position, even before you are promoted. Then, write action statements that reflect the outcomes that represent superior performance in the position."

"I sort of get what you're saying, but can you help me understand what exactly those statements need to look like?"

"Sure. I'll give you three ideas right now, because almost all jobs have three universal components that reflect superior performance."

Emily poised her pen above her notebook. "Fire away."

"One key result might be to have a clearly defined and communicated plan for success in your department. So, you're giving people clarity about what pathway you're taking and how it aligns with the organization's strategy. Almost every leadership role has some version of that key result."

Emily finished writing and looked up at David expectantly.

"A second key result that reflects superior performance might be that you achieve or exceed all of the tangible, measurable goals for the coming year. Those goals could be financial or they could be tied to specific milestones. The point is it's something with clear metrics."

"Hmm. So, for my team, maybe that's launching a certain number of successful software updates in a quarter?"

"Exactly."

"For your role as CEO, what's an example?"

"Company revenue was probably my biggest one. But my job was to make sure that revenue wasn't the only thing shareholders paid attention to. I had my team keeping a close eye on employee productivity, safety, and satisfaction. Number of work days missed, injuries, production stalls—those types of things. We also paid close attention to customer metrics, including how many customers we kept, or how many we lost because of a problem we weren't able to solve. And there are a lot of other statistics or metrics that come into play when you're the CEO of a company."

"OK, so, let me make sure I've got this." Emily looked at her notes. "The first key result might be a clearly defined and communicated plan for success. The second key result could be tied to something measurable."

"Right. And the third key result that's universal to most leadership positions is to develop and advance the value your team provides to the company."

"What do you mean by that?"

"Well, your team represents a certain level of expertise. We know expert leadership is defined by creating value for others, continuing to add to that value, and expanding your expertise. So, the idea behind this key result is: How do you continue to develop the capacity of your team to create new or different value in the future? One way is by continuing to strengthen the culture of your team."

"Culture. I've heard that term a lot, but it seems sort of ambiguous."

"For most people, it *is* ambiguous. As a CEO, nurturing the culture was one of the most important things I was responsible for. My definition of culture became the values, assumptions, and beliefs that governed our organizational behavior. I guess you could call it organizational character."

"The values, assumptions, and beliefs that govern behavior. Can you give me an example?"

"Sure." David lifted his eyes to the ceiling in thought. "OK, I've got one. When I was CEO, I did a strategic planning session with my core executive team, and we worked together to define the things that were important to them in how they wanted to work as a company. They ended up with three statements: We play it straight; we don't play games with people. We treat trust as a preferred currency of relationships. We use systems and processes to achieve excellence.

"Those are examples of values, assumptions, and beliefs that drove how we did business and provided a lot of insight into decision making. By aligning our decisions with those statements, we were able to quickly identify good and bad ideas."

"I like that. I'm going to start a conversation within my team to define the things that are important to them in how we work as a team."

"Great plan. So, those are three really clear key results you can build on. Do those help?"

"They do," Emily replied, setting her pen down. "But they seem a little . . . imprecise. How do I know if I'm achieving them?"

"Good point," David said. "In a way, you can think of those three to five key results as being the strategic plan for your position as director. Once you have a strategic plan, you can put together an operational plan that answers the questions: How am I going to measure each of these key results? What are the metrics I'm going to use? And with those metrics in place, you can build a schedule. You can define dates and deadlines, assign tasks—create a highly detailed plan. But all of that is the expression of the strategic key results."

Emily studied David for several seconds. "This is incredible stuff, David. I've never thought about my career, my work, this way. Where did you get all this?"

"Decades of reading, applying, and leading."

"Amazing." Emily looked down at her notes. "OK, can I recap integrity in positional leadership to make sure I got it right?"

"Of course."

Emily scanned her notebook. "First, understanding and following the rules of the position. Second, measuring expected key results—and I guess not just measuring, but defining those key results and then achieving or exceeding them. That's two. One more, right?"

"Yes," David said, taking a drink of his coffee. He made a face. "Time for a warm-up. Join me?"

"Sure."

They walked down the stairs and to the counter, handing their cups to the barista.

"Dark roast, please," David said.

"Decaf for me," Emily added.

The barista looked at Emily. "Not up for caffeine acrobatics today?" she said, nodding toward Emily's belly. "Every time I had coffee when I was pregnant, my son seemed to do karate."

Emily laughed, admiring the barista's cap-sleeve green summer dress and messy chic hair. "Yeah, this kid, too. I've cut back caffeine entirely, but decaf is almost as good, right?"

"Almost," the barista said with a wink.

Emily and David returned to their table. As Emily took her seat, she noticed David's face flush. "You OK?" she asked.

"Yes. I'm good," he said, but he seemed to be struggling to catch his breath.

"Are you sure?" Emily said.

"I'm fine. Really."

"Let me get you some water."

Emily fast-walked back downstairs, filled a glass of water, and hurried to the table.

"Here you go," she said. Her brows were furrowed in concern. "Can I get you anything else?"

"No, no. Don't worry. I'm old. This is what happens when you age."

"Ah, but you're only in your seventies. I need my body to work when I'm that age. I've got a lot of traveling to do."

David laughed, coughed, and took a sip of water. "I bet your body will hold up better than mine. You're more active than I was. Now where were we?"

Emily decided to let her concerns go. He looked fine now and obviously wanted to move on. "We were just about to cover the third aspect of integrity in positional leadership," she said.

"Oh, yes. The third way to define integrity in positional leadership is how you manage the relationships that are specifically connected to your position as director."

"What do you mean?"

"Well, obviously you're going to need to manage your relationship with your boss appropriately, to take responsibility for building the right kind of relationship. Which, by the way, you've already done."

"I have?"

"Your conversation with Mitchell demonstrates taking responsibility for managing that relationship the appropriate way. Oftentimes, in leadership, we think we're managing down, but you're actually going to spend a lot more time managing up. And as a matter of fact, that's what will earn you more and more influence in the organization—managing up with integrity and continuing to keep logic in front of emotion. The leaders above you will learn to respect and admire you. They'll ask you for more and more help when you continually manage up with integrity."

"Managing up. Got it. And obviously, managing relationships with the people on my team is really important, too."

"Absolutely. And remember, our definition of integrity is all the parts working together to create a desired outcome and result, so each of your team members must understand just as clearly as you do what integrity looks like for their positions. They need to also know the three to five key results that reflect superior performance for their roles. And you have to give them feedback so they understand where they're at, how they're doing, and what they can get better at."

"There's that 'feedback' word again. For some reason, every time I hear it, something inside me tightens up." She noticed her shoulders creeping closer to her ears, so she sat up and relaxed her upper back.

"Yeah, it's too bad that's how most people feel about feedback. A lot of times, I think that's because we don't understand how to build integrity in relationships when it comes to feedback."

David went on to share about a study he'd read from the University of Washington about relationships. The researchers video-recorded couples for eighteen minutes, and they were given a set of questions to talk about. After studying numerous couples, the researchers were eventually able to predict whether or not a couple would be together in five years, just by watching the way they talked to each other.

"I read that study a while back," Emily said. "Enlightening, huh?"

"Yes, and if you recall, they discovered that for spouses, there's a behavior that gives them a 92 percent chance of staying together."

"That's right. I can't remember the specifics, though."

"It's the number of times a person demonstrates kindness or respect compared to the number of times they criticize their spouse. Do you remember the ratio?" Emily shook her head, so David continued. "Five to one. Now, that doesn't mean that if you don't hit five, your marriage is going to fall apart. What it means is that if you can consistently demonstrate kindness and respect five times for every one negative interaction, there's a 92 percent chance you're going to have a successful marriage."

"I find that so fascinating. And do you see how that study could apply to the workplace, too? Is that where you're going?"

"As a matter of fact, research indicates that in the workplace, the ideal ratio is three to one—three interactions of kindness and respect for every one criticism. The reason so many people tighten up at the word 'feedback' is because they don't recognize that praise, affirmation, and endorsement are also forms of feedback. So, when your boss gave you positive affirmations in your conversation with him, did it make you feel differently about him by the time you left?"

"Definitely. It shifted my perspective of him."

"That's part of integrity in relationships with your team. One of the responsibilities you have as a director is to guide their career, work, and performance. Their success becomes your success. And if they fail, to some extent it becomes your failure. You need to give them every possible chance to succeed, and that means you need to help each person understand how you're going to measure their performance, and then provide regular feedback. And I'm suggesting that if they're the right person for the job, at least three pieces of feedback you give them should be positive for every one that's corrective."

"That's such actionable advice," Emily said. "For my career, and for my marriage."

David nodded. "I have more to share. You OK on time?"

"My morning is clear."

"Great. So, the last piece of relationship integrity in a position is with the people who are your peers. This is maybe one of the toughest, because the person above you is fairly easy; you know you need to please them. The people below you are fairly easy; you know they need to please you. But your peers—other directors or people in the company you don't have a direct reporting relationship to—this is where you can get into trouble if you're not thinking about building integrity."

David explained that integrity in relationships with peers begins by being gracious. But just as necessary is being helpful, whether or not you are getting credit. Always making others feel comfortable sharing ideas and opinions is another aspect of integrity, too—never cutting people off, demeaning them, or being condescending to them. Applying the same three-to-one ratio is important.

"You should aim for people to feel energized and heard after they interact with you," he added.

"What a powerful way to look at my relationships with others."

"I think so. Energizing others really shifts the way you engage."

"I can see that." Emily glanced at her notes, scanning the page. "OK, so integrity in positional leadership is defined by rules, results, relationships," Emily said. "Catchy."

"I hadn't noticed that," David said with a grin.

Emily nodded, returning a smile. "I'm not going to ask your advice about this one. I'm going to do my own assignment of discovering what the rules, results, and relationships will be for the director position."

"Great plan."

The two sat for several minutes, drinking their coffee, chatting about the news and family. Emily was overcome with gratitude as she looked across the table at the older gentleman who had helped her clean up her coffee several months earlier. She was pretty sure David felt grateful, too—how could he not? What they'd found in that coffee shop was special. It was indefinable, nonsensical, strange, and life-changing.

—

Later that night, Emily stared in disbelief at her phone. It was 8:57 on a Saturday night—she'd almost made it a full day without checking her email, but she'd finally caved after helping clean up dinner and putting Henry to bed. And there it was, among industry newsletters and non-urgent colleague requests, an email with the subject line: "Congratulations! You've been nominated for Women in STEM!"

Her throat caught in a half-swallow as she clicked the message open with her thumb, scrolling down as she read it.

Congratulations, Emily,

You've been nominated by Alex Vanil at Enertec for the 9th annual Women in STEM awards! This award is given to remarkable women in Idaho who exemplify strong leadership in the fields of science, technology, engineering, and math.

Your nomination is recognition of your influence in your community and beyond. The next step is to apply. Please send your application by July 3. A panel of peers and former honorees will review all applications and announce recipients July 10.

Again, congratulations on this honor. You should be incredibly proud.

Sincerely,
Rebecca Baylor
Women in STEM Awards Director

Emily blinked. She reread the email. Alex? Mitchell's boss? Sure, she saw him a few times a month for team meetings, but what had motivated him to nominate her?

Emily looked at the clock. It was just after nine, and she'd get to sleep in until eight thirty before heading to prenatal yoga the next morning—assuming Henry slept in too, of course. She reached her arms up, tilting her body slightly backward and hooking her arms behind her head. She stared at the ceiling for nearly a minute before her mouth corked into a half-smile. Alex. Maybe she was beginning to gain influence within her company.

Was it her character? Expertise? It certainly wasn't her position.

Returning her body back to an upright position, she stood, set her phone on the table, and made her way into the kitchen, where Jason was making popcorn for a movie they were going to watch together.

"Jason," she said. "You're never going to believe this."

"I bet I will."

She laughed. "I was nominated for Women in STEM—you know, that award they give out every year? The one my old boss, Joan, won a few years back."

Jason's face expanded in surprise and joy. "Emily!" He walked toward her and wrapped her in a hug. "Emily, that's amazing!"

Emily held him for a moment before drawing back to meet his eyes. "It's just a nomination. But wow, pretty cool, huh?"

"Very cool."

She picked up her phone, which still displayed the email. "I need to fill out an application by—oh, boy. By Wednesday. Not much time." Emily pulled up the award website and navigated to the application page. "It looks like the application window has been open for six weeks, so I'm on the tail end. They've already started reviewing submissions." She looked at him. "I mean, is it worth applying? I bet they've basically picked the recipients by now."

"You'll get it done, and you'll knock their socks off. I can take

Henry out to lunch and the park tomorrow so you can have the house all afternoon. That way you can work on it uninterrupted."

"Really?"

"Really."

She leaned over and gave him a kiss on the cheek. "Ready for our movie?"

"Yep." Jason picked up the popcorn bowl and followed Emily into the living room. They settled into the couch, the popcorn within arm's reach on the table in front of them. With a few clicks of the remote, the movie started playing.

Later that night, it took Emily a full half hour to fall asleep, her mind racing, trying to think of exactly why Alex would nominate her. She had no doubt it had to do with her work with David.

David, she thought, her heart quickening in the still, dark room. I can't wait to tell David.

She rolled over, placed a hand on her husband's back, and closed her eyes, imagining the STEM stage and what it might feel like to be honored for her influence. As she fell asleep, she envisioned Henry and her, hand in hand, walking across the stage, beaming as Henry accepted the award on her behalf.

9

What Great Leaders Do

mily tapped her fingers rhythmically on the table. It was the Monday after receiving the Women in STEM nomination email, and she'd arrived at Slow by Slow, unannounced and unplanned, to share her exciting news with David.

She glanced at her watch. 7:36. It was time to head into work, but she wanted to give him a few more minutes. Maybe he was just running late. Or perhaps he'd switched from every day to just a few days a week. They'd been meeting on Saturdays for so long, she really didn't know his routine anymore.

At 7:41, she finally stood and walked downstairs. She handed her empty coffee cup to the barista.

"No David today?" the barista asked.

"Nope. Has he been in like usual?"

"Every morning," she replied as she placed Emily's cup into the bus bin under the counter. "Well, now that I think about it, he misses a day every now and then."

"Oh." Emily felt slightly relieved. "Any idea why?"

"I think he's been exercising," the barista replied with a grin. "He always looks winded when he comes in here. I'm guessing his wife has him on a walking regimen."

Emily laughed. She envisioned Dania picking out stylish workout clothes for him. "Well, that makes me feel better."

"I'm sure he'll be in tomorrow."

"Tell him I said hi, will you?"

"Will do."

Emily made her way outside to her bike. The July heat had crept into the early morning, and as Emily pedaled to work, she felt dampness begin to kiss her forehead. By the time she arrived at work, she decided to take a short walk to cool down before heading inside.

She locked up her bike and began walking the block that circled her building, watching the cars drive by. Inside were almost all single-commuters, likely making their way to work. She spotted a gray sedan across the intersection stopped at a light, an older gentleman in the passenger's seat and a slightly younger woman in the driver's seat. Emily squinted behind her sunglasses. David!

Just as she began to wave hello, the two drove by, leaving Emily to wonder if David's late coffee shop arrival was because his wife was accompanying him. She smiled to herself, happy to see them together. So that's what he's been up to: spending time with his wife.

Emily turned back in the direction of her work, deciding not to take the full loop around the block and instead heading upstairs. As she boarded the elevator, she took a deep breath. Good things were coming. She could feel it.

—

Two Saturdays later, Emily rode her bike through downtown Boise toward Slow by Slow. She'd been disappointed when David rescheduled their last meeting, but at the same time, maybe it was better this way. There was no sense in sharing a nomination, right?

Once her bike was parked and locked, she walked inside and was surprised to see David waiting for her upstairs. She'd arrived ten minutes early, expecting to procure a table for them. But there he was, smiling and waving in her direction. She nearly skipped over to him.

"David!"

He stood, and they hugged. "I'm glad to see you," he said.

"Me too. Do you want some coffee?"

"Is my name David?" He winked.

"So, yes to coffee."

"Yes."

Once coffee was ordered and on its way, they spent a few minutes catching up. Emily held back until she felt like she was going to burst.

"I have news," she said.

"More news than a baby and an inevitable promotion?"

"More news," Emily said, looking down at the table briefly. She was surprised to find she was a little embarrassed to share her excitement with someone other than Jason. "I am an honoree for Women in STEM."

"Emily," David said. He reached across the table to take her hand. "Emily, that's . . . that's . . . I don't know what to say other than congratulations. You deserve it."

"Thank you," she said, squeezing his hand and then letting go. "And I'm hoping you'll sit at my table, as my guest. The ceremony is two Thursdays from now."

"I'd be honored," David said.

"It would mean a lot to have you there."

"It would mean a lot to be there." He cleared his throat, his eyes shining with emotion.

Emily swallowed and blinked, trying to hold back her own emotion, but with no luck. Two tears fell, and she wiped them away quickly. She said nothing, letting the moment lengthen. Finally, she said, "I think the thing that most surprises me is who nominated me. It was Alex Vanil, Mitchell's boss. I didn't even know he noticed me beyond our weekly meetings."

"That doesn't surprise me at all."

"It doesn't?"

"Not even a little," he replied. "Think about what you've been working on. You've been building your influence by focusing on what you can control 100 percent. You've been collaborating with others through your monthly celebratory lunch. And you've been putting your concerns into the right context, focusing on developing your own version of a PhD rather than worrying about a potential acquisition. And by doing all that, you've been gaining new influence over the areas you have concern about."

"That's true. I've been called out by Mitchell in three separate meetings to comment on women in tech."

"Exactly. Alex noticed you because you're beginning to exercise influence in areas you didn't know you had influence, and those areas have grown considerably over the past several months."

Emily was quiet, replaying team meetings with Alex in her mind. Maybe Alex did see her as influential in the company.

"And then your character," David went on, "you've been taking our conversations seriously and building character intentionally with great focus. You've been establishing positive habits, focusing on your values, and openly seeking other people's feedback. People are also beginning to notice you're the smartest person in the room because of your commitment to being a good expert leader.

"At the same time, your commitment to humility has helped you to present your case with more diplomacy and respect, and to not act like you're the smartest person in the room, which can be an easy trap to fall into when you *are* the smartest person in the room on a particular subject." His eyes met hers, as if to make sure she understood what he was saying. "Remember how I told you to forget the position and it will come to you? Well, I can tell it's not very far away."

Emily was quiet. She thought about the last few months. It was the hardest she'd ever worked on herself, really focusing on her growth and the advancement of those around her. Every aspect of her life had improved. Work was better, yes, but home? That was probably the best part. She felt focused and energized at work, and engaged at home. She'd long since stopped checking work emails in the morning before leaving the house, choosing instead to be present with Jason and Henry, and she'd implemented a "no tech" rule from 6 to 8 p.m. every night, the precious window she had with her family. Anchoring to her value of presence, she knew, helped her stay focused on protecting that time with her family. There was a new sense of hope that maybe, just maybe, she could be fully present at work and at home. Perfection? No. But she was becoming a better human, and that's what mattered most.

"Honestly, I don't know how much better it can get," she said. Her voice was soft as she tried to verbalize her thoughts. "Except maybe that director position. And yet, it feels so much less important than it did a few months ago."

"I'm really happy for you, Emily. I'm thrilled to see how engaged you are and how much you're enjoying life."

"Thank you. Me too. And it's all thanks to you."

"It's not. But I'm happy to play a small part. You did the hard work."

"That's true. I did, didn't I?"

David nodded. "I do want to offer some caution."

Emily sat up, surprised. "Oh?"

"Position, expertise, and character are always a work in progress. It's very important that you realize you're not finished. You're not even close to being finished. None of us are. Great leaders who make the most of their opportunity never have the attitude that they've arrived."

Emily was listening intently. "Go on."

"You're about to face one of your greatest challenges as a leader: success. The question is, will your success create complacency? And that complacency won't be obvious because you're too smart for that. It will be almost imperceptible, so subtle that only over time will you be able to look back and realize that you'd unknowingly become complacent in continuing to build your character and expertise. The things that derail us are rarely big; they're usually nearly invisible, and they'll steal your energy over time."

"How do I avoid that?" Emily said. "How do I keep from becoming complacent?"

"One way is to always come back to the things great leaders do," he replied. "You've already been doing them. Now, you just need to continue, and become more and more intentional about doing them over time."

"Things great leaders do," Emily said, thinking over the many topics they'd covered. "Have we covered those already?"

"Not yet. May I?"

"Please."

"Well, the first thing great leaders do is turn problems into opportunities. In fact, they realize their purpose is in large part about solving problems."

"Something to look forward to," Emily said with a grin.

David went on to explain that while most people think of problems as just being the hassles of life, or hindrances that keep them from enjoying success, great leaders don't view problems that way. Instead, to them, problems open up new pathways that never could have been accessed without those problems appearing.

"Are you familiar with Napoleon Hill?" he asked.

"The journalist? Yes."

"Well, I was really impacted by his work, and while I didn't always agree with his conclusions, one thing he wrote has stuck with me to this day. He said, 'Every failure, every adversity, every heartache carries with it a seed of an equal or greater benefit.' I've been trying to prove that quote wrong since I heard it, but I haven't been able to, so I'm convinced that great leaders look at a problem and see opportunity others don't."

Emily paused in thought. There was a weight in David's words that hadn't been there in previous conversations, like he was trying to impart wisdom that would carry her to the late stages of her career.

"You know, I can see examples of that in my own life. In fact, not getting a promotion is what spurred all of this"—she opened her arms wide, as if enveloping the entirety of their relationship and work together—"and to me, not being promoted was a big problem I didn't know if I'd ever solve. And actually, I'm still a manager. Maybe I'll never solve that problem. But it's what got us talking, and it was the trigger, the catalyst, that's helped me grow so much over these past several months."

"Great insight. Ready for the next one?" David said. Emily nodded. "Great leaders inspire people to make commitments they wouldn't otherwise make. And Emily, this is one of the greatest satisfactions you'll get as a leader, when someday you can look back and see how you challenged or affirmed someone, and they took the next step and the next. You'll get great joy out of playing a part in their success by inspiring them to make a commitment they wouldn't have made otherwise."

The two looked at each other for a meaningful few seconds. As much as she'd benefited from her relationship with David, she now understood just how impactful it was to him, too. But would she ever have such a profound effect on someone she leads?

"That's hard for me to imagine right now," she finally said. "I'll have to trust you on this one."

"It's not something you set out to do intentionally most of the time. It usually happens because someone is watching you when you don't realize it. A young leader will watch your character and the values by which you choose to govern yourself, and she'll decide she wants to treat other people that way. Or she'll observe your passion for learning and getting better, avoiding complacency in spite of success, and decide to learn, too. There will be times when you encourage or inspire intentionally, but most of the time, you'll inspire without ever realizing you've done it."

Emily had been taking notes and stopped abruptly when a wave of nausea hit. "Excuse me for a moment?"

"Of course."

Rather than heading to the bathroom, Emily made her way outside. Maybe the fresh air would help. She pulled a sour pregnancy candy out of her pocket and popped it into her mouth, then interlaced her fingers on top of her head, looking around at downtown Boise. The city was abuzz with energy, mostly families and couples milling about, enjoying the cool weather before temperatures skyrocketed to 100 or more later that day. After a few more breaths in and out, Emily felt better. She wanted to make it through this conversation and be present. For some reason, she felt like this might be the most important conversation they'd had so far, even more than character.

Moments later, she sat down across from David. "Sorry about that."

"No need to apologize," he said. "I've been through this with my wife six times, remember?"

"Ah, yes. An old pro," she said. "Now, what else do great leaders do?"

"There's one more thing." David's eyebrows furrowed slightly, his posture straight, hands folded on the table in front of him. He held an aura of importance, and she knew to listen carefully to what he was about to say. "They transcend self-interest and self-promotion. What captures their attention and passion is bigger than themselves."

"Hmm. So, are you saying those things are bad? Because I feel like a lot of what I've been doing has to do with self-interest and self-promotion."

"They're not bad. They're just not enough."

"What do you mean?"

"Self-interest and self-promotion are necessary at times, but great leaders never stop there. They find something bigger, and their own interests suddenly become a distant second to what motivates them. Instead, they're driven by the opportunity to make a difference."

Emily sat in thought, processing what he'd said. She wanted to be that leader, and she didn't want to take another decade to get there.

"I know my cause, my purpose that transcends self-interest and self-promotion," she finally said. "It's to reach back and help other women take the same journey I'm taking. It's to not do it alone—to bring others along with me." After a long pause, she added, "Or maybe not just women. I want to help anyone who aspires to be a great leader. Why should I limit myself to women? I am a mom to a boy, after all. I want to support all people who strive for excellence."

"All people," David echoed. "Well said."

Emily looked down at her notes and read aloud. "Turn problems into opportunities. Inspire people to make commitments they wouldn't otherwise make. Transcend self-interest and self-promotion."

"Good summary. I have no doubt you'll live up to those and

maybe even add another measure of what great leaders do. Now, I'd better get going. Breakfast date with my wife."

The two stood, and Emily walked next to David as they made their way outside.

Before they parted, Emily stopped and turned to face him. She willed herself to be present emotionally. She needed to get this out.

"David . . ." she began, trailing off as she gathered emotional strength.

"Yes?" he said.

"I just—I want you to know how much I appreciate our time together. These mornings, they're . . . they're what I needed. I have grown so much. I've come to love you like family."

David looked at her quietly. "I feel the same. These mornings have revitalized me. They've opened me up. Even my wife has noticed." He laughed. "So, thank you, Emily. I've grown to love you like family too."

They hugged and parted, David to breakfast with his wife and Emily to meet her husband and son at the park. They'd agreed that, in lieu of their next meeting, they'd see each other at the awards ceremony.

Emily turned just in time to see David disappear around a corner. She smiled to herself, taking in the morning, reflecting on the past several months. David was a gift. And now she knew she was a gift to him too.

It's Time

Emily stood in the lobby, clutching her phone in her right hand and staring at the set of doors that led into the building. The award ceremony attendees had long since filed into the ballroom, and she could hear the emcee speaking.

She smoothed her dress, a long, elegant black gown she'd found at a boutique maternity shop. Her hair was expertly styled in loose curls, and she'd even had her makeup professionally done. Jason had insisted she be pampered in preparation for the ceremony; in addition to pre-awards styling, he'd gifted her a massage and manicure.

The day had been perfect. Until now.

The thing she'd been looking forward to most for the past two weeks was spending the evening with Jason, David, and Dania. Her parents hadn't been able to attend due to a prebooked trip to Montana.

Where is he? She checked her phone again. Why hasn't he emailed or called?

She'd sent her number to him earlier that evening, just in case they couldn't find each other in the crowd, but hadn't heard back. This wasn't like him. Yes, he was a few minutes late occasionally, but to not show up without getting in touch? Surely he hadn't forgotten.

Music escaped through the closed ballroom doors, and Emily reluctantly made her way toward the event, turning around every few steps to look at the building entrance. With a deep sigh, she pulled open a door and quietly made her way between tables to where Jason was sitting. She slid in next to him and glanced at the two empty chairs to her right. Her throat tightened.

"Any word?" Jason whispered.

"Nothing," Emily said, her voice barely audible.

Jason placed his arm over her shoulders and pulled her in for a close hug. "I love you," he said into her ear. "This night is about you. I'm sure David will come, and if he doesn't, you'll get to tell him all about it next time you meet."

Emily said nothing. She rested her head on Jason's shoulder and closed her eyes, willing herself to be present. Finally, she opened her eyes and righted her head, looking toward the stage, where the keynote speaker was finishing her talk. Applause erupted, and the sound washed over Emily like water, and with it, her worries about David were gone.

Half an hour later, Emily was standing behind a large curtain to the left of the stage. She listened for her name, and then walked to the stage to accept her award. As she stepped onto the platform, she heard a loud cheer in the audience and looked out to see a lone figure standing in the crowd. It was Jason, whistling and clapping like she'd just been named president of the United States.

She accepted her award, shook hands, and posed for a picture. Jason was silent now, watching her. He only sat down after she finally exited the stage.

When she arrived back at the table and took her seat, he leaned over. "I'm so proud of you," he said.

She reached out and grasped his hand, saying nothing. The tears were back, threatening to spill down her face, a mix of gratitude for her husband and disappointment at David's absence. She swallowed, kissed him, and turned her attention to the front.

As she watched the other recipients accept their awards, she knew the award itself wasn't what mattered. She could have been accepting a box of macaroni instead of a trophy. But she felt deeply about this honor because of the story behind it: the months she'd spent working on herself; the evenings and weekends she'd leaned on her husband to take on more parenting and household duties; the friendship she'd developed with David; the celebration she'd spurred at work; the evolving relationship with Mitchell; the influence she'd gained simply by growing herself; the shift she'd set in motion for women in her company by how she handled her own experience with discrimination. It was the effort, the continual quest to become better, that made tonight so special.

David wasn't here, but he was the catalyst. She would find a way to celebrate with him, to share how deeply she'd been impacted by his investment in her as a person.

"Jason," she said. He turned to look at her. "Thank you for being here."

He nodded, wiping a stray tear from her cheek. He picked up her trophy, a small statue of a woman holding a star, turning it over in his hands in admiration.

She studied the award. "You know, I think I'll give that to David."

"Great idea. Except I'm sure he won't accept it." He handed the trophy back to her. "After all, you earned it."

She set the trophy on the table, and they turned to watch the emcee close out the evening.

—

"Morning," Emily said to the barista, walking past her toward the stairs.

She'd stopped into Slow by Slow on her way to work, hoping to catch David. There had been no word from him since he'd missed the awards ceremony the past Thursday. Before ordering, she walked up the steps to survey the near-empty seating area, then made her way back downstairs.

"Decaf drip. To go, please," she said, distracted. She was staring out the window, watching people walk by and looking for David.

"No David today?" the barista said.

Emily shook her head. "Have you seen him?"

"Not this week," she replied. "I was on vacation last week, so I'm not sure if he was in."

"Right." Emily handed over her debit card. The barista ran the card and turned toward the back counter to pour Emily's coffee.

"Don't worry, this is totally normal," she called over her shoulder to Emily. "He almost never comes in on Tuesdays anymore."

"Yeah, OK." Emily bit her lip. "I'm meeting him here on Saturday, so I can talk to him then. Will you let him know I came in when you see him?"

"Sure thing."

Before leaving, Emily took three steps up the stairs to scan the space once more. No David.

It was early still, so she decided to leave her bike locked in front of the shop and walk to work. She closed her eyes for a few steps, breathing in the late summer air. There was nothing like Boise in the summer.

Taking a detour through the center of downtown, she stopped at the Boise Centre fountain. Recent construction had turned her little town center into one that felt metropolitan. She barely recognized the place where she'd spent childhood summers splashing in the fountain. At the next street, she took a left, heading in the direction of work. In less than ten minutes, she was riding the elevator in her building, exiting at her floor, and finally, standing outside her soon-to-be-vacated office.

This was the news she'd been so excited to share with David that morning: She'd been recruited for a vice president position at another company. In just three short weeks, she'd leave Enertec and begin a new career journey.

To be honest, she'd wrestled with the decision. She'd been surprised when Lynn, the senior vice president of information technology at a local startup, approached her after the awards ceremony the week prior. The startup was a booming company that had grown 200 percent in the past three years, with a charismatic CEO known for his work ethic and drive for excellence. When the SVP had asked her to an early coffee meeting the next morning, she'd enthusiastically accepted. The job offer came later that day. There had been no application or interviews. They wanted her that badly. And apparently, Lynn had been watching Emily's work for several months.

She'd been dumbfounded at the offer. Grateful, but overcome. In that moment, she remembered David's words. Her position was a stewardship. It was something she would never own.

The recognition felt extraordinary. But after all this time at Enertec, and all the progress she'd made at the company, leaving felt . . . what? Risky? Like she was leaving something unfinished? It was hard to say goodbye to her colleagues, friends, and the work home where she'd spent much of her adult life. Still, she knew it was the right choice for herself and her family. She felt like she'd done what she could at the company. It was time to move on and explore new possibilities.

Emily opened her office door and turned on the light, remembering the meeting with Enertec's CEO the previous morning. After spending the weekend thinking over the offer and talking with Jason, she'd set an appointment with the CEO, in which she told him she was resigning. In that meeting, he'd asked if there was any way she would change her mind, even offering her a VP position at Enertec that beat her new salary and benefits. They'd talked for nearly an hour, and when he'd finally realized she wasn't budging, he'd said he understood and wished her well. As she'd walked to his door, she stopped and turned to him.

"One thing before I go," she said. "If my leaving does anything, I hope it's this: You'll find ways to promote more women here. Things are shifting—I know that. But it needs to continue."

"You can count on that. I promise you." The CEO was standing in the middle of his office, looking at her with purpose. She held his gaze before closing the door behind her.

But that was yesterday, and now it was Tuesday. While she was proud of her decision and excited about her new role, one thing wasn't right: Why hadn't she heard from David? She'd emailed him that weekend as she grappled over her decision and even called his cell. Sunday afternoon, she'd finally received a text from David's phone that said, "Emily, this is Dania. I'll call soon."

She walked toward her chair, laptop bag still over her shoulder. Suddenly, her movements halted. She stared at her desk. On the surface sat a small envelope with a single word, written in scrawling cursive: *Emily*.

She set her bag down, gently picking up the letter and surveying it for a moment. The envelope was made of fine cream-colored paper, thick, with a grain that reminded her of custom stationery. She ran her fingers over the surface, then flipped it over to reveal a red wax seal, stamped with the letter "D." Emily touched the wax gently; she'd never seen a real wax seal before.

Finally, she slid her right index finger under the flap and carefully opened the envelope, pulling out three handwritten pages.

Setting the envelope down, she leaned against her desk and began reading.

Dear Emily,

For the past few months, I have been battling brain cancer, one that didn't respond to chemo, radiation, or alternative

treatment. The doctor says I only have about two weeks left. I've asked Dania to give you this letter after I pass.

I hope you can understand why I didn't tell you. One of my values is resiliency, and to me, that means that even in the face of the hardest things in life, I want to retain my dignity. Dignity meant getting to live the last months and days of my life not as though they were my last but instead as the continuation of a full and happy life. It is important to me to say goodbye to the people I care about, and this letter is my way of saying goodbye to you.

Emily, you have brought me new life. Just when I was facing the reality of death, you spilled coffee in a little shop in Boise, Idaho, and gave my days deeper meaning. The time we spent together—the discussions, the coffee, the celebrations—those are special to me.

I know great things are ahead for you. Greatness is ahead of you. I see in you fierceness and tenacity. I wish I could be there to see you bloom.

The last time we were together, I gave you caution; this time I want to give you courage. Your future extends beyond where you can likely see right now, and as you continue your journey, the path you're meant to take will become clear. Your greatest final act of leadership will be giving what you've learned to someone else.

Lastly, Emily, I want you to know I believe in you. I believe in what you can do and who you can be. I believe in you as a leader. I believe in you as a mom. I believe in you as a friend. I believe in your ability to make a difference in this world, because, Emily, you made a difference in mine. You helped make my final days useful.

Love,
David

Emily looked up from the letter. She was emotionless. Numb.
David was . . . dead. Dead? No.

No. He couldn't be.

With sudden force, unstoppable tears covered her cheeks. Sadness and anger mixed with the realization that she would never get to say goodbye. He'd never know what he'd helped her achieve.

He was gone. David was gone.

How had she not known he was sick? Or had she? Did she choose to ignore his sunken eyes and pale skin, to not notice his slow pace and persistent cough? Was she so caught up in what he had to teach that she didn't notice his body failing him?

Emily shook her head. It didn't matter now.

She stood, unmoving, his letter to her chest, tears dropping to the floor, quiet sobs escaping her lips.

Memories ran through her mind like a film reel. The spilled coffee. The walk on the greenbelt. Sitting at the long table at Slow by Slow. Henry's birthday party, talking under the willow tree. And their last interaction, when they'd hugged goodbye and she'd watched him disappear around the corner.

Why hadn't she walked with him? Why hadn't she extended that moment just a little longer? She struggled to remember his last words to her, replaying the exchange in her mind over and over, grasping for specificity. Suddenly, she remembered: "I've grown to love you like family too."

Family. She thought of Dania, and a shiver washed through her body. She needed to go to her. Emily remembered the text she'd received two days earlier. Had her emails and calls been coming in as David left this world?

How selfish she'd been, staring at David's empty chair at her awards ceremony. She should have known everything was not all right. She should have left and found him to say goodbye.

Emily shut her eyes tight, letting the tears and loss encompass her. She needed to feel his absence in its fullness.

Finally, there were no tears left, and she stood in her office, staring blankly. Silently, she folded David's letter and carefully slid it back into the envelope. She would take the day to remember him, and she knew where to go. Pulling out her phone, she composed a text.

"I need you," she wrote to Jason, "Meet me at Slow by Slow?"

His reply came fast. "On my way."

⸺

Emily sat at her desk, staring across the room at nothing in particular. Two months. It had been two months since David passed, and yet the ache was still there. She thought of him during weekly coffee at Slow by Slow, which she now spent with her husband. She did constant double-takes of silver-haired men and had reread his letter at least two dozen times. She'd visited Dania, bringing her meals and flowers, picking up groceries and mowing her lawn.

Still, that emptiness. Would it ever go away?

She was busy enough at work and home that she edged him out of her mind most of the day. It was in the still of night, with Jason lying next to her and Henry asleep in his room, that she remembered.

A light tap on Emily's door yanked her out of her thoughts. She looked at the slides she was finalizing for an executive presentation later that day, then toward the source of the sound.

"Yes?"

"Emily?"

Emily stood. "Yes?" she repeated.

"I'm Jacqueline," the young woman said, taking a few steps into Emily's office. "I'm new. I was just hired into your management training program."

"Jacqueline," Emily echoed. She walked around her desk, extending a hand. "Nice to meet you. What can I help you with?"

"I've been following your work," Jacqueline said. She spoke fast, nervous. "I hope that's not strange. I was just . . . I'm wondering if we could maybe sit down sometime? I'd love to ask you some questions."

Emily paused. There was David again, a memory skittering across her consciousness of the day she'd anxiously asked him to meet and share his knowledge. Then, her thoughts scanned forward to her last discussion with him, remembering what she'd said that morning: *I know my cause, my purpose that transcends self-interest and self-promotion. It's to reach back and help other women take the same journey I'm taking. It's to not do it alone—to bring others along with me.*

"I'd be honored," Emily said.

Jacqueline's expression relaxed. "Great. I'll look forward to it."

Emily surveyed the woman's face. She was younger than Emily

had realized, probably fresh out of college, ready to take on the world. With Emily's help, maybe her world would be full of more opportunity and promise than Emily's early career years had been. Thanks to David—no, thanks to her hard work with David as her guide—she was creating a new future for the young leaders she was fortunate enough to influence.

"There's a coffee shop I love called Slow by Slow," Emily finally said. "Why don't we meet there tomorrow morning at seven?"

"I'll be there," Jacqueline said, then hesitated. "Would it be OK if I bring my colleague, Angelo, with me? He's been following your work too. I told him I'd ask."

Emily paused, remembering the rest of what she'd said to David: *Or maybe not just women. I want to help anyone who aspires to be a great leader.* She smiled at Jacqueline. "Of course."

Jacqueline thanked Emily and said goodbye, shutting the door behind her.

Emily walked back to her desk. She pulled open her top drawer and withdrew an envelope with her name written in cursive, lifted it to her heart, and looked around her newly acquired office.

"This is because of you, David," Emily said into the emptiness. "This is because of us."

Holding the letter to her chest, she placed her right palm on her abundant middle, wondering if her baby would be anything like his namesake.

Acknowledgments

First and foremost, I'm grateful to Stacy Ennis for her partnership on this book. You have been wonderful to collaborate with and your contributions have been vital to telling this story. I admire your writing skills and the way you live your life, and I'm better because of knowing and working with you.

One of my best advisors over the past decade has been Maryanna Young of Aloha Publishing. Thank you, Maryanna, for helping me understand the publishing industry better and for supporting all of my writing adventures.

The Greenleaf Book Group has been fantastic to work with throughout the entire process. To Emilie Lyons, Justin Branch, Tyler LeBleu, AprilJo Murphy, Karen Cakebread, Kim Lance, Chelsea Richards, Kristine Peyre-Ferry, and Jen Glynn: Thank you for bringing us under your wing and for helping us "dress" this story with the best editorial inputs, title, cover, design, and on and on.

The team at Price Associates and our clients continue to inspire me to get better. It was their encouragement that convinced me the time had come to tell this story after years of sharing these ideas with leaders in many countries. I'm particularly grateful to Andy Johnson for convincing me we had something to share and to Nichole MacDowell for her tireless contributions as our director of communications and PR.

Finally, I'm immeasurably grateful to my wife, Pam. She has been patient, caring, and supportive beyond anything I deserve. Thank you for letting me follow my passion and for all the sacrifices you have made so I can share my ideas around the world.

—Ron

Writing this book with Ron Price has been one of the most meaningful experiences of my career. Much in the way Emily learns from David, I got the opportunity to sit with Ron for days, drinking tea with him in his office, asking questions, and listening. Ron, I've grown as a leader and writer, with a stronger commitment to my values and greater awareness of my impact on those around me. Thank you for your investment in this process. And thanks, Pam Price, for the delicious tea.

The team at Greenleaf Book Group, mentioned earlier by Ron, has been a joy to work with from start to finish. Emilie Lyons opened the door for this book to happen, and I'm truly grateful to her. To the entire team, thanks for believing in our book.

There are several people who invested significant time and energy into reviewing the manuscript: Brent Patmos, Alecia Hoobing, Jennifer Belt, Mindy Bortness, Dorien Derksen, and Nichole MacDowell. Each of you played a significant part in shaping the content. Donna Cook and Frieda Johnson both served important roles in the editorial process. Thank you all.

And finally, to my husband, Doug, and my kids, Lily and Max, thank you for inspiring scenes in the book and supporting me as I holed up in my office to finish drafts. You three fill me up. I love you.

—Stacy

Resources

For more information and resources from the book, including chapter notes, a full values list, and more from the authors, visit www.price-associates.com/growinginfluence.

More titles by these authors:

Reader's Guide

1. Did you enjoy the story of *Growing Influence*? Would the story have been more or less impactful if it was written as nonfiction?

2. What are the most valuable insights you gained from this book? Why are they important to you?

3. Were you able to connect or relate to any of the characters? If so, who and why?

4. How did the book affect you personally? Did reading it help you focus more on professional growth? Did it inspire you to reflect on the kind of leader you want to be in the future?

5. Do you experience frustration in your career? Do you think the lessons in this book could help overcome these frustrations and obstacles?

6. What tools from this book will you implement in your life to improve your career?

7. What are the five values by which you govern yourself? What

are the five values by which you relate to others? How well do you think you live by your values?

8. What does the ability to influence mean to you? What about integrity?

9. There are three areas of influence: control, collaboration, and concern. What examples of the areas of influence do you see in your life, and how can you grow within these areas?

10. Since the lessons in this book apply to everyone, how do you think having a woman as the protagonist impacted the story?

11. How are the three different types of leadership—character, expert, and positional—present in your life and work? What areas of leadership can you improve in?

Q&A with the Authors

1. **What compelled you to write this book? What inspired you to write it as fiction instead of nonfiction?**

Ron Price (RP): I have spoken on the topics in the book for several years. One of our team members, Andy Johnson, kept encouraging me to write a book about these concepts because he felt they were original and impactful. As I reflected on this, I concluded that the models of leadership would be better communicated through a work of fiction. Originally, I asked Stacy to serve as the executive editor/ghostwriter. It quickly became obvious to me that she should be credited as a coauthor. This book could not have been completed without her valuable and original contributions.

Stacy Ennis (SE): I've worked on a number of leadership books over the years, all of which have been meaningful. However, I'd never worked on fiction within the genre of business and leadership, and the idea was both exciting and challenging. One of the things I enjoyed about writing this story with Ron was pushing ourselves to explore a new way to communicate leadership lessons that can profoundly affect people's lives and careers. Developing the story with Ron stretched my creativity and helped me grow as a leader, and I can't wait to see the impact it has on others.

2. **Did you discover anything new in the process of writing this story?**

RP: We always discover new things through the process of writing! We decided early on that framing our leadership insights within the context of gender bias would be valuable. Then the #metoo movement happened and elevated the importance of what we were doing.

SE: I agree with Ron—we learned a lot about the content and characters, and we also saw the importance of the story play out in the media as we were writing the book. But more than that, I learned the power of conversation around leadership as Ron and I dug deep into the concepts of the book. We recorded hours of discussions as we teased out ideas and explored different pathways for interpretation and implementation by readers.

3. **What was the most rewarding experience throughout your book-writing journey? What has been the most important or beneficial lesson you have learned?**

RP: Collaborating with Stacy has been a very rewarding experience for me. She is an extremely skillful writer and represents a set of experiences I value but will never have myself. Though we come from very different backgrounds, we share many values. Once again, I have been reminded of how little I can do alone and how much better my writing projects are when I collaborate with talented people.

SE: Working with Ron on this book taught me what it looks like when you bring two perspectives together to create something bigger than we could create on our own. Ron is one of the most values-driven, ethical, hard-working leaders I know, and he's also a great listener. As we watched the #metoo movement unfold alongside revising this book, we had great conversations about what it means to be a woman in business. He modeled empathy and understanding, which I strive to bring into my own leadership.

4. **What were the biggest challenges you faced cowriting a book? What were the biggest rewards?**

RP: Scheduling was our only real challenge. I am extremely busy with our work, including traveling up to 70 percent of the time. Working on the book took place after normal business hours. Stacy was patient and responsive throughout the process. The biggest rewards are seeing a result that neither of us could have created alone. Participating in the creative process is always one of my greatest joys. In my opinion, writing fiction with purpose is a delicate venture, and I'm thrilled with OUR end result.

SE: Ron's response makes me smile, because he was extremely on top of revisions—truly an ideal coauthor! As someone who writes around two and a half books a year, the greatest challenge was stepping outside of my normal nonfiction process to work with Ron in creating Emily's and David's characters and telling their stories. The biggest reward? Even after all these rounds of revision, I still tear up when I read the last chapter. To me, we did the story and content justice.

5. **What makes your book unique from other books on leadership?**

   RP: The models we write about are unique to us, and they have been tested and validated for more than forty years. They are an extension of the work we do understanding and encouraging leadership excellence.

   SE: I'll echo Ron, though the leadership lessons are his. I helped refine and expand them, but they are concepts he's developed over decades. Our book is also unique because it brings together two voices from different backgrounds and life experiences to tell a single story, which will allow a wide spectrum of readers to be able to connect to the characters and lessons.

6. **The lessons that David shares in the book, where did they come from? Were they lessons you learned through your own careers, saw through others' careers, or researched?**

   RP: David's lessons come mostly from my experiences and work with other leaders—much of the book is autobiographical. There are also several special touches I am thrilled with from Stacy's experiences.

SE: Ron's stories are present throughout the book. You'll see some of my life through Emily's experience, especially when it comes to her parenting. Some of the discussions Ron and I have had also made it into the book through David and Emily.

7. **What would you say is the most important message or lesson to take away from *Growing Influence*? Why?**

RP: If I had to narrow it down to one message, it is that everyone is a leader, and their influence is made up of a combination of character, expertise, and position. Intentional leaders think about building integrity in all three dimensions based on their individual passions and purpose.

SE: I'll add one thing to Ron's response: all leaders have the opportunity for growth, no matter their current situations. The message of intentionality extends to the decision to grow.

8. **Is there anything else either of you wanted to include in this book that you may have not had the chance to?**

RP: This book captured everything I was hoping it would. Because this is an extension of earlier books (*The Innovator's Advantage, The Complete Leader,* and *Treasure Inside*), I view it as part of my journey reflecting on leadership. There may be one or two more books in the future to complete my sense of responsibility in sharing these reflections with others. There are so many wonderful books about leadership, it is impossible to acknowledge all of the authors I admire and benefit from reading. That said, our team members at Price Associates have authored several books that are near the top of my list (http://price-associates.com/store).

SE: As a writer, I would love to explore a more complex version of this story. Since this is a business fable, we made intentional choices to keep the story in support of the lessons.

9. **What are your plans for the future? Will you write another book?**

RP: I hope to write at least two more. I have spent the last five or seven years working on content through speeches and conversations with leaders that I hope to use as the basis for my future writing. I have been working on a new approach to strategy, developing practical keys to effective supervision, and using value theory (axiology) as a management practice. I hope that I can eventually craft my thinking around these topics into books that benefit others.

SE: One thing I'm especially excited about is a women's leadership platform training I cofounded with three other incredible women (http://nextlevelwomenleaders.com). As for writing another book, my answer is *definitely*. I've been writing regularly since grade school, and I don't plan to stop writing anytime soon. I also look forward to publishing more books under my name, as many are ghostwritten.

10. **Do you identify with any of the characters? If so, who and why?**

RP: Both David and Emily! I probably identify more with David because much of his story is my story in disguise. However, Emily's experience also has autobiographical aspects as well.

SE: I identify with both characters as well, though probably more so Emily. As a mom of two young children, her challenges balancing family with career certainly resonate with me. My husband is also an all-in father and constant support to me, much like Emily's husband, Jason.

11. **What kind of research did you do for this book?**

RP: Over forty years of reading thousands of books, then implementing what I was learning in my experiences, and finally working with scores of emerging leaders as an executive coach and program facilitator. Because I develop my thinking about a topic for at least five years, my research happens along the journey much more than during the writing process.

SE: I love research and spent a lot of time listening to podcasts about women in business, leadership, and more, as well as reading articles and books. Like Ron, I'm an avid reader and have spent more than a decade refining my thinking around the concepts we explore in the book.

About the Authors

Ron Price is an internationally recognized business advisor, executive coach, speaker, and author. Known for his creative and systematic thinking, business versatility, and practical optimism, Ron has worked in fifteen countries and served in almost every level of executive management over the past forty years. As the former president of a multi-million-dollar international company, Ron works shoulder-to-shoulder with executive leadership teams to bring strategic clarity and transformational results to organizations. In 2004, Ron started Price Associates, and he serves as president and CEO of the global leadership advisory firm that focuses on helping organizations grow in the areas of leadership, innovation, and culture. Ron is also the creator of The Complete Leader Program, an EMBA-style learning experience that has been used by organizations around the world to grow leadership skills and character. Learn more at www.price-associates.com.

Stacy Ennis is a creative consultant, success coach, speaker, and writer, as well as the cofounder of Next Level Women Leaders, a leadership training company. Her background includes leading as the former executive editor of *Healthy Living Made Simple*, a Sam's Club magazine that reaches around 11 million readers, as well as serving as the longtime ghostwriter for a Nobel Prize winner in medicine. Stacy has written or edited dozens of books, including her own book, *The Editor's Eye* (Night Owls Press, 2013). Her TEDx talk, *How to Raise Brave Kids*, has been viewed thousands of times by people across the world. She has a master's degree in professional writing and editing from the University of Cincinnati and a bachelor's degree in writing from Boise State University. Learn more at www.stacyennis.com.